For my wife, Heather

Published in The United States in 1999 by
Contemporary Books
A division of NTC/Contemporary Publishing
Group, Inc.
4255 West Touhy Avenue
Lincolnwood (Chicago), Illinois 60646-1975 U.S.A.

ISBN 0-8092-2594-8

Managing Editor Kate Bell
Editorial Assistant Tanya Robinson
Copy Editor Norma MacMillan
Editorial Consultant Jenni Muir

Art Editor Alison Fenton
Stylist Wei Tang
Food for Photography Meg Jansz
Typesetting Olivia Norton

Picture Research Liz Boyd
Production Julian Deeming

Cataloging-in-Publication Data is available from the
United States Library of Congress
Printed in Hong Kong

Page 1 *Mango Sorbet (page 106)*
Pages 2–3 *Mother-in-Law's Eyes (page 107)*
Pages 4–5 *Married Shrimp (page 32)*

café brazil

Michael Bateman

Photography by Jeremy Hopley

CB

CONTEMPORARY BOOKS

Contents

Introduction

Brazil is the land of exuberant Carnival and the insistent rhythm of the samba. Its colorful people love the pleasures of life, music, dance, and food. Especially food. From the tropics of the Amazon north, which yield a cornucopia of exotic fruits, to the gaucho south where they rear cattle, Brazilians enjoy a rich and varied cuisine. Nowhere is this more evident than in this huge country's street food. At any public event, food sellers materialize, peddling everything from freshly simmered corn-on-the-cob to colored hard-boiled eggs.

Brazil has been a melting pot of food cultures from the sixteenth century onward, a fusion of the food of the native Indians, the Portuguese colonizers, and African slaves. Later, in the nineteenth century, other waves of immigrants added their contributions, first Italians and Spanish, then Poles and Lebanese, and, more recently, Japanese. São Paulo, one of the world's biggest cities, with a population of 17 million, boasts the largest Japanese community outside Japan, and is home to literally thousands of *sushi* bars. And Italian pizza and pasta have become universal fare both in homes and in cafés.

Brazil is the largest country in Latin America, on a par with the United States in terms of size and population. The diversity of climate from north to south equates with the differences between the damp Loire Valley and the steaming rain forests and arid deserts of West and Central Africa. So in the south, you find cowboy types grilling steak over charcoal fires (the *churrascaria*), while in the north, the meat eaten is more likely to be *carne de sol* or *carne seco* (beef salted and dried in the sun). In the north, though, they enjoy a wealth of Amazon fish, wild game from the forest, vegetables such as chayote and jícama, and exotic fruits such as *graviola* (the succulent custard apple), *jabuticaba* (a cherry-sized acid fruit with a jellied texture), breadfruit, jackfruit, and carambola or star fruit, not to mention papaya, mango, pineapple, guava, and passion fruit.

Of all the fruit and vegetables that Brazil produces and exports none are more important than beans. Brazil is the world's largest grower and the biggest consumer. Black ones, brown ones, red and white ones. The small black beans *(feijão preto)* are the most prized. Beans and rice are eaten by most families every day, and the national dish (which Rio lays claim to) is *feijoada*, a rich, liquid stew of black beans in which half a dozen or more kinds of meat are submerged. *Feijoada* is colorfully served with white rice, butter-yellow *farofa* (the toasted meal milled from cassava), green stir-fried kale, and rounds of sliced orange. It is traditionally preceded by a searingly strong rum sour called *caipirinha*, made with chopped limes crushed with sugar.

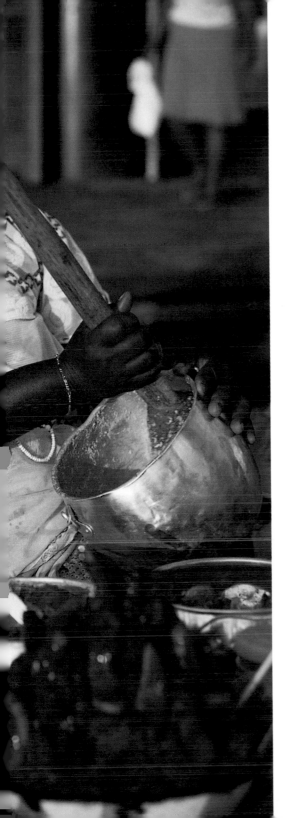

Brazilian food might have been a modest cuisine had it not been for the contribution made by the Africans, former slaves. Emancipated in the 1880s, they have made Bahia, their homeland in the northeast of Brazil, a byword for imaginative cooking. What we see in Bahia is an early example of fusion cooking. The Portuguese came to Brazil, annexing the produce of the indigenous Indians – limes, avocados, corn, sweet potatoes, pumpkins, pineapples, and peanuts. And for their part the Portuguese brought European foods—rice and sugar, olives and olive oil, cilantro (the universal Brazilian herb), and, above all, the pig, and thus cured hams and sausages and lard for cooking.

The Africans in their turn introduced several kinds of palm from West Africa, one producing palm nut oil *(dendê)*, a thick, reddish, highly saturated oil that contributes perfume and flavor to any dish cooked with it. Another palm, the coconut palm, provides its multi-purpose nuts, which contain a liquid *(água de coco)* that is a very refreshing and cooling drink on a hot day. The white grated flesh and the milk made from it feature in both savory and sweet dishes. And, since the hot northeast is alien to the growing of wheat, the Africans, needing a starchy base for subsistence, brought over cassava, a hairy, white-fleshed root as thick as a coffee mug. The meal when toasted is called *farofa*, and is sprinkled like a condiment on many dishes.

So it was that, when these several food cultures and all these disparate ingredients met, there was a gastronomic "big bang" and *Cozinha Baiana* (Bahaian cuisine) was the result. The most popular dishes are based on seafood and shellfish – fish soups (with coconut milk, lime juice, cilantro, and hot chilies), simple fish stews *(moqueca)* with sliced onion, tomatoes, and bell peppers, dyed yellow with *dendê* oil, and the local specialty, baked stuffed crab, *recheadas de siri*.

Hot chilies are in evidence here, usually incorporated in the food, while in other parts of Brazil freshly made hot chili sauces or *salsas* are always served at the table. They are mostly made from the *malagueta* chili pepper, a witheringly hot, very small variety native to Brazil.

Sweet dishes are adored in Brazil and served at every meal. A breakfast spread in Le Meridien hotel, in Copacabana, offers not only a dozen ripe tropical fruits, but rich caramel *pudim*, coconut flan *(quindão)*, cooling *manjar blanco* (a delicious wedge of blancmange made with coconut milk), succulent breads made with cornmeal, banana, and coconut, and unusual preserves called *cocadas* – caramelized beets, carrot, pineapple, mixtures of pumpkin and coconut, guava paste, quince paste.

The recipes chosen for this book only begin to touch on a wide-ranging, vibrant, and exciting cuisine that is Brazil's. Read, taste, enjoy.

The Brazilian pantry

Abóbora *The Brazilian orange-fleshed pumpkin has a dense, firm flesh, similar to butternut and kabocha squashes. It can be eaten on its own, added to soups and purées, or made into pie fillings and desserts.*

Avocado (abacate) *Brazil has many varieties of avocado, from smooth to rough-skinned, small to very large. Avocados are enjoyed in savory salads, but also, unusually, as a dessert, the flesh creamed with sugar and then chilled.*

Banana *In the markets you see bananas of every shade of color and every size. Some are actually plantains, only used in cooking. These are usually cut into sticks and shallow-fried.*

Beans (feijão) *Feijão preto (black beans) are the most prized, being used in the national dish. They are small and as shiny as black pearls when first washed, and cook to a thick, coal-black purée. They are sometimes sold as turtle beans. The more common bean is a beige-brown bean called* mulatinho. *The black-eyed pea (fradinho) is used to make acarajé, crispy fritters flavored with ground dried shrimp.*

Cachaça *A white rum, also known as* aguardente, *made from sugar cane. Numerous varieties exist, of every quality, from fire water to premium brands. In Rio de Janeiro, a restaurant called the Academia da Cachaça stocks 2,000 varieties, the oldest from 1875.*

Cassava (mandioca or macaxeira) *Also called manioc and yuca, this starchy root contains poisonous toxins and must be processed to remove these before drying and grinding. The meal (farinha de mandioca) is coarse, like cornmeal (you can find it in Latin American and Caribbean markets). When toasted in a dry pan it becomes known as* farofa, *and as such it is sprinkled on many foods in the northeast, rather like a condiment. When fried in dendê or butter to make it yellow, it is called* farofa amarela. *Another variety of cassava,* aipim, *contains little poison, mostly in the skin, and is edible after cooking. Aipim is sold in markets to be used just like potatoes, boiled or fried. Tapioca is derived from cassava, and tapioca flour is called cassava flour.*

Chayote (xuxu) *This green, apple-sized vegetable, also known as mirliton or christophine, is much liked in Brazil. When boiled it has the character of cooked cucumber, and it is often baked in a cheese sauce. It also works well in chilled salads with onions and fruit, providing a crunchy texture.*

Chili pepper (pimenta) *Pimenta-do-cheiro ("cheiro" means aroma) is a tiny, round, red or yellow chili, half the size of an olive. Pimentas-do-cheiro are normally bottled in a mild vinegar. Pimenta malagueta, Brazil's seriously hot chili, is similar to Caribbean or Scotch bonnet peppers. Both red (very hot) and green (not quite so hot) are served at the table either bottled or in freshly made sauces, with most meals. Malaguetas are also bottled in vinegar, in oil, or in cachaça, or blended with liquid from a stew or soup. Brazilian cooks use little hot spicing in the preparation of a dish, leaving the amount of chili heat to be added by individual diners to taste.*

Chorizo (chouriço) *The blanket name for all kinds of cured sausage, sometimes mild, sometimes piquant, sometimes smoked. Chorizo is often fried and then added to bean stews. Lingüiça is a long sausage, usually sold doubled into a u-shape.*

Cilantro (coentro) *This is the most popular Brazilian herb, used freely as an ingredient and a garnish.*

Coconut (côco) *Green, or unripe, coconuts are sold by the roadside, split in front of you with a machete and served as a refreshing drink. The flesh can be scraped away like creamy paste. Once mature, the coconut, now brown and hairy, is used in cooking. The liquid inside, água de côco, is lovely for* drinking, and the white flesh, grated, is a key ingredient in desserts, pastries, and cakes, as well as being used to make coconut milk, essential in many seafood stews and countless other savory dishes.

Dried salt cod (bacalhau) *Imported from northern waters, bacalhau is part of the colonial Portuguese tradition. It must be soaked overnight in several changes of water to remove the salt, but then it needs only brief cooking, after which it must be carefully boned and skinned. The flesh is mixed with onion and tomato in savory purées and stews, or with a starchy base such as potatoes to make croquettes and bolinhos, little deep-fried balls.*

Dried shrimp (camarão seco) *An essential but pungent ingredient in Bahia, this is used like a condiment to impart a salty, seafood flavor. Fishermen moisten the shrimp with dendê oil before laying them to dry, and half fry, in the burning sun for several days, raking them over from time to time.*

Graviola *Also called fruta do conde, pinha, or ata, this is similar to the custard apple or cherimoya. It looks like a large, green-skinned, closed pine cone. The custardy flesh, tasting of pears and melons, is used in desserts after the shiny black seeds have been removed.*

Guava (goiaba) *The guava is loved for its perfume and tart flavor. It is used in drinks and sorbets, and to make*

a paste called goiabada, eaten at breakfast with white cheese.

Kale (couve) *The most important hearty green vegetable in Brazil, kale is always eaten with a Saturday* feijoada, *finely shredded and stir-fried.*

Lime (limão) *Brazil has no lemons, and* limão *is often mistranslated as lemon; however, its vivid green color and powerful fragrance soon make it clear that the* limão *is a (superior) world away from other citrus fruits. It is essential in most Brazilian dishes, not least in the cocktail* caipirinha.

Mango (manga) *Originally brought from India, the mango has truly acclimatized itself to northern Brazil, where the abundant fruit crashes down from huge trees the height of oaks.*

Okra (quiabo) *In Bahia, okra is also known as* cararu– *the name given to an okra and dried shrimp purée.*

Palm hearts (palmito) *Harvested and canned, these are the size of the white of large leeks, and not unsimilar in their silky texture. An obligatory hors d'oeuvre or salad ingredient in Latin America, palm hearts harmonize well with delicate seasonings and dressings.*

Palm nut oil (dendê) *Deep yellow or reddish, thick, and strong-flavored, this is the cooking medium of the northeast.*

It is not one of the world's most healthy vegetable oils, being as highly saturated as animal fat.

Papaya *Also known as paw paw, these have an unmistakable rich perfume when ripe. Larger varieties are known as* mamão *and have lurid orange flesh. Best served with a squeeze of lime juice.*

Passion fruit (maracujá) *This is probably Brazil's favorite flavor in drinks. The yellow, red, and purple* maracujá *seen in markets are much bigger than those sold in the U.S., more tart in flavor and slightly less perfumed.*

Pineapple (abacaxi) *Native to Brazil, fresh pineapple juice makes sublime alcoholic drinks such as* batida, *mixed with the white rum,* cachaça.

Sun-dried salted beef (carne de sol) *This is bought in salty chunks and needs to be soaked overnight in several changes of water to get rid of saltiness before it is used for stews.*

Ingredients illustrated on previous pages
Top row (*left to right*) cassava meal and cassava; black beans and black-eyed peas; dried salt cod and dried shrimp; limes; pineapple; kale and cilantro.
Middle row (*left to right*) graviola; dendê oil; chorizo and lingüiça; tapioca flour and tapioca pearls; pimenta-do-cheiro and pimenta malagueta; coconut and palm hearts.
Bottom row (*left to right*) mango and passion fruit; papaya; chayotes; bananas and plantains; white rum (cachaça); guavas.

The Brazilian kitchen

Cooking the Brazilian way requires no mystifying pieces of equipment, neither strange-shaped pots or pans nor bamboo basket steamers, neither special knives nor chopsticks.

In Brazil's southern states, the outdoor cook will be at home, because much of the meat is cooked on a grill, or *churrascaria*, a technique that requires no more than a pair of tongs and, in the case of the Brazilians, a mug of salted water to splash on the meat (this prevents the meat from producing a hard, resistant crust, so it cooks through better).

In the big cities, such as São Paulo and Rio de Janeiro, cookware is straightforward: large saucepans for cooking beans, smaller saucepans with tight-fitting lids for rice, and deep ceramic casseroles into which beans and meat are sometimes decanted to finish cooking in the oven. Hefty wooden spoons and potato ricers are essential too, to mash cooked beans for soups and sauces, plus various forms of sieve to make them into purées.

Most homes will have a pressure cooker for beans, which reduces the cooking time from 3 hours or so to about 30 minutes. There will be at least a once-a-week bean cook-up. The first beans will be eaten as they are. The next day they are usually heated up, fried in oil or lard, and mashed (*refritos*—literally refried). Subsequent servings see them return in the form of purées and soups.

The oven is much used, both for the baking of savory pastries and for the numerous sweets, custards, flans, and fruit breads. But the wide range of dishes, molds, and cake, bread, and tart pans is no different from those used anywhere else. The frying pan is essential, too. Chicken croquettes, shrimp with their shells on, *picadinhos* (little pieces of meat), and pork cracklings *(torresmos)* are all cooked to a crisp in the frying pan. A *frigideira* is an iron ovenproof frying pan that can be used both on top of the stove and in the oven.

Many of the *salgadinhos* (bite-sized snacks) emerge from the deep-fryer, such as the *bolinhos* (deep-fried balls of shrimp, ham, salt cod, and rice). The deep-fryer is even more essential in the northeast where the unique cooking of Bahia derives much of its character and flavor from the use of the thick, orange-colored palm-nut cooking oil, *dendê*. Street sellers set up a deep pan of simmering oil on the sidewalk and deep-fry the little bean fritters, *acarajé*, to order.

In some regions you find specialized pots. In Minas Gerais, for example, they use black stoneware casseroles for a *tutú à mineira* (their version of a *feijoada*, in which the beans are mashed to a purée). In the Amazon north, off the island of Marajoara, they use two-handled, tall terracotta vessels that resemble Roman amphorae.

A tough grater, or the grater attachment on a food processor, is a vital kitchen utensil, given the importance of grated coconut in Brazilian cuisine. Screwdrivers and hammers are best suited to dealing with the shell. Roasting split coconuts for 30 minutes in a hot oven develops the flavor and makes them easier to grate.

Food processors and blenders have taken the place of the mortar and pestle for many basic Brazilian kitchen techniques, especially in the northeast—making mushy purées, pounding soaked black-eyed peas for *acarajé*, and pounding dried shrimp. But the mortar still has its place in every kitchen, and is always used to mash avocados or to break up chopped limes for a *caipirinha*.

Tropical fruit is an essential part of the Brazilian table, so a juicer has to be a good investment. The health-conscious Brazilian consumes vast quantities of fruit and vegetable juices, either on their own (a *suco*), as a milk shake (a *vitamina*), or mixed with alcohol (*batida*).

Making coconut milk

Coconut milk—the creamy liquid extracted from the grated flesh—is one of the most important ingredients in Brazilian cooking. If you cannot get fresh coconuts, it is easy to make with dried shredded coconut. Or use one of the prepared coconut products on the market, the best being coconut milk in cans. Coconut milk powder is also available.

To make coconut milk using a fresh coconut, first pierce holes in two of the three indented "eyes" at the base of the nut using a hammer and large nail or tough screwdriver. Pour out the liquid into a container, straining it through a sieve or cheesecloth to remove any dust or debris from the shell. To open the shell, find a good hard surface and, using a hammer, tap the shell firmly and repeatedly across the middle until it breaks apart. Use a heavy, blunt knife to separate shards of flesh from the shell, then cut off the hard brown skin from the pieces of flesh.

It can be painful work to grate coconut flesh using a household grater, so it's preferable to use the grater on an electric mixer or food processor. An average coconut will yield about 6–8 ounces (about 2–3 cups) grated coconut flesh. Put the grated coconut in a bowl and pour on ½ cup hot but not boiling water. Leave to soak for 10 minutes. Then line a sieve with cheesecloth or a cotton cloth and pour the soaked coconut into it. Gather up the ends, fold them over, and squeeze out the liquid as if you were wringing out a T-shirt. Set this liquid aside.

Repeat the process, using 2 cups hot water. This will produce a thinner but still tasty liquid. Mix together the first and second pressings and you have 2½ cups of coconut milk. If you leave it to stand, a layer of thick "cream" will rise to the surface, and this can be skimmed off and used for a richer result.

(Canned coconut milk will also separate in this way, so the can should be shaken before opening, unless you want the richer cream from the top.)

To make coconut milk with dried coconut, use 1 heaping cup coconut with 1 cup hot water for the first pressing and 1½ cups water for the second pressing; this will yield 2 cups coconut milk. Or use powdered instant coconut, allowing ¾ cup to 2 cups water to make the same volume.

Below *Shrimp Pastries (page 28)*

SOUPS
AND APPETIZERS

Stuffed Eggs

Ovos Recheados

Some dishes that originated in Europe—where they have all but died out—live on in Latin America, and none more so than stuffed eggs. They appear in many guises among the varied appetizers that are offered on celebratory occasions. In Bahia, ovos reacheados may be served with Coconut and Shrimp Cream (page 79) and a dusting of Golden Cassava Meal (page 72). Ovos recheados can be filled with many appetizing stuffings, such as shredded tuna in mayonnaise spiced with malagueta *chili, garnished with halved green or black olives or a sprinkling of chopped parsley or fresh cilantro.* **Makes 16**

8 free-range eggs

2 tablespoons grated white bread crumbs

½ cup freshly grated Parmesan or other hard cheese

2 tablespoons butter *melted*

sea salt and freshly ground black pepper

1 Preheat the oven to 400°F.

2 Hard-boil the eggs for 4–6 minutes. Peel under cold running water. When cool, cut in half lengthwise. Set the whites aside and put the yolks in a bowl.

3 Pound the egg yolks, mixing in the bread crumbs, cheese, butter, and a seasoning of salt and pepper. Using a teaspoon, form the mixture into neat shapes similar to egg yolks, and stuff the egg white halves.

4 Place in a baking dish, cover with foil, and heat through in the oven for 10 minutes.

Chicken Soup

Canja

Every country has its nourishing chicken soup, which is intended to bring comfort and solace. Brazil is no exception. **Serves 6–8**

1 Place the chicken in a large saucepan and cover with 2 quarts water. Add the onions, 2 of the carrots, the tomatoes, celery, cilantro or parsley, celery leaves, peppercorns, and salt.

2 Bring to a boil, skimming off the scum that comes to surface. Turn down the heat and simmer for 2 hours.

3 Remove the chicken from the broth and, when cool enough to handle, remove and discard the skin. Pull the meat from the bones and cut into strips. Strain the broth, discarding the vegetables, which will have passed on their goodness to the broth. Return the chicken meat to the saucepan along with the rice and the remaining carrots.

4 Bring back to a boil and simmer for a further 30 minutes. Season to taste before serving.

1 stewing chicken

1 pound onions *quartered*

4 carrots *sliced*

**1 pound fresh ripe tomatoes or
1 x 16-ounce can whole tomatoes**
drained and seeded

2 stalks celery *sliced*

**small bunch of fresh cilantro or
parsley** *chopped*

3–4 celery leaves

12 black peppercorns

1 teaspoon sea salt

½ cup long-grain white rice

Pumpkin Soup
Quibebe

Although abóbora, *the squash used for this soup, translates as "pumpkin," it is not the watery giant Halloween vegetable. The Brazilian pumpkin is a dense-textured member of the squash family. The close texture and rich, sweet taste of this squash make it attractive for both sweet fillings in desserts and savory soups such as this, beloved of the African community of Bahia.* **Serves 6**

1 Halve the *abóbora*, remove the seeds and fibers with a large spoon, and pare away the hard peel. Cut the flesh into bite-sized chunks, about 1 inch square.

2 Heat the oil in a frying pan and cook the onion until it softens and starts to turn yellow. Add the garlic and cook for 1 more minute. Stir in the chili to heat through. Finally, add the tomato and tomato paste. Heat, stirring, to blend the flavors thoroughly, then transfer to a saucepan.

3 Add the *abóbora* pieces and the stock to the saucepan and bring to a boil. Turn down the heat to low, cover with a lid, and simmer for 20–30 minutes or until the *abóbora* breaks up into a purée. Whisk it with a fork or put in a blender or food processor briefly. Add salt to taste and stir well.

4 Serve with chili sauce and grated cheese, to be added as you like.

2¼ pounds *abóbora* (or use butternut or kabocha squash)

4 tablespoons *dendê* oil (or use olive oil or butter)

1 onion *minced*

1 garlic clove *crushed, then chopped*

1 fresh hot red chili pepper *sliced into fine rings* **(optional)**

1 large tomato *skinned, seeded, and chopped*

2 teaspoons tomato paste

3½ cups chicken or beef stock

sea salt

To serve:

Tabasco or West Indian chili sauce

grated Cheddar or Parmesan cheese

Golden Chicken "Legs"

Coxinhas de Galinha

Appetizers (salgadinhos) *that have been breaded and then deep-fried have a long European tradition. The Brazilians are masters of this preparation, too. Every sort of mixture—based on potatoes, cassava, vegetables, fish, beef, pork, or chicken—can be assembled to make croquettes, rissoles, and such like.* Coxinhas *are bound with a pastry skin, so they don't fall apart in cooking.* **Makes about 12**

corn oil

3½-pound chicken *cut into 8 pieces*

½ onion *minced*

1 garlic clove *crushed, then chopped*

sea salt and freshly ground black pepper

white bread crumbs for coating

For the dough:

1½ cups rice flour

2 cups milk

7 tablespoons butter *softened*

3 free-range egg yolks

few drops of chili sauce

To serve:

Chili Salsa (see page 21)

1 Heat a little oil in a Dutch oven or heavy-bottomed saucepan and brown the chicken pieces on both sides. Add enough water to cover the bottom of the pot, then cover and cook gently until the chicken is tender, 20–30 minutes. Drain, reserving the cooking juices for the dough.

2 When the chicken is cool enough to handle, pick the meat away from bones and skin (they can be used in stock). Cut the breasts into 12 long strips—they will be the core of each *coxinha*. Mince or grind the remainder of the meat and mix with the minced onion, garlic, salt, and pepper.

3 In another bowl, mix the rice flour with the milk and enough of the reserved chicken cooking juices to make a stiff dough. Mix in the butter and the egg yolks to make a soft dough. Stir in the minced chicken. Season to taste, adding a little chili sauce.

4 Divide the dough into 12 equal lumps. Take a piece of chicken breast and roll a piece of dough around it, forming into the shape of chicken leg. (Some cooks reserve pieces of chicken bone and push a knobby end into each shaped piece to simulate the leg bone and serve as a useful handle.)

5 Roll the shaped pieces in bread crumbs. Deep-fry in hot corn oil at 350°F, in batches, until golden brown all over. Drain on paper towels, and serve hot with the Chili Salsa.

Cheese Croquettes

Croquettes de Queijo

Among the most common snacks in Brazil, these are served at any time of the day, from breakfast to supper. Smaller versions can be served as part of a mixed presentation of salgadinhos. **Makes about 12**

1 Preheat the oven to 350°F.

2 In a bowl, rub the butter into the flour, then mix in the egg yolk followed by the bread crumbs, cheese, and a seasoning of salt and pepper. If the mixture is too dry, add a spoonful of water to help bind it together. Shape the mixture into balls slightly smaller than the size of an egg.

3 Oil or butter a baking sheet. Whisk the egg white lightly in a bowl, dip each croquette into it, and place on the sheet. Bake for 25–30 minutes or until brown and crisp, checking if the croquettes are cooked after 20 minutes. Serve hot with Chili Salsa.

4 tablespoons butter *diced*

1 cup all-purpose flour

1 free-range egg *separated*

½ cup fine dry white bread crumbs

½ cup freshly grated Parmesan or other hard cheese

sea salt and freshly ground black pepper

Chili Salsa

A small saucer of this salsa (molho de campanha) accompanies almost every main dish in Brazil, be it meat grills, stews, fish, beans, or rice. In a bowl, mix together 1 red onion (or any mild onion), chopped into small pieces, 1 large tomato, skinned, seeded and diced, 2 tablespoons red wine vinegar, 1 garlic clove, crushed and then chopped, 2 tablespoons olive oil or sunflower oil (optional), 1 tablespoon chopped fresh cilantro or flat-leaf parsley, a few drops of malagueta *chili oil or other chili sauce, and salt and pepper to taste. Taste and adjust the seasonings to get a good balance of hot, salt, sour, and smooth. Chill for 1 hour or so, to allow the flavors to blend. For molho apimentada, add a ladle of liquid from cooked beans, or a stew. For molho de limão, use the juice of 2 limes instead of red wine vinegar.*

Corn Parcels

Pamonha de Milho Verde

The most common street food in São Paulo, this is a tasty corn mixture wrapped in its own husks and steamed. Unsweetened, with a little salt added instead of sugar, these are also served at parties with other appetizers, and may be eaten warm or cold. They must be made with fresh, not canned, corn. **Makes 16**

8 young ears of corn in their husks

½ cup milk

sugar to taste

1 tablespoon butter *softened*

1 Remove the ears of corn from their husks, reserving all the green leaves but discarding the silk. Separate the best 8 inner leaves.

2 With a grater, shred the corn kernels off the cobs into a bowl. Drain the grated corn, then put it into a blender. Add the milk and blend until quite smooth and thick. Sweeten to taste, and beat in the butter.

3 Divide the mixture into 8 equal portions using a tablespoon. Shape each portion into a ball and wrap in one of the inner leaves. Fold the two long edges inward, to enclose the mixture, then wrap the ends over to make a tight parcel. Tie with kitchen string or fasten with rubber bands.

4 Line the top half of a steamer with the outer leaves of the corn husks and place the parcels on top, seam side up. Steam for about 50 minutes, or until the husks have turned yellow. Make sure the water doesn't boil dry beneath them.

5 The stuffing will be quite sticky, so you need to leave the parcels to cool for 15 minutes before serving.

Little Cheese Custards

Queijadinhas

Mixtures of sweet and savory are typical of Brazil. These little mouthfuls of a sweet-savory custard are baked in tiny wax-paper cases such as are used for petit-fours. They will keep for a few days in an airtight tin or in a plastic container in the refrigerator.

Serves 6 (makes about 24)

1 x 15-ounce can condensed milk

2 free-range egg yolks

1 cup freshly grated coconut
(or use shredded dried coconut)

2 teaspoons freshly grated
Parmesan cheese

1 Preheat the oven to 400°F.

2 In a bowl, beat together the condensed milk, egg yolks, coconut, and Parmesan with a wooden spoon.

3 Fill 24 wax-paper petit-four cases with the mixture. Lay a sheet of foil in a wide baking pan and set the cases on the foil. Fold up the sides of the foil all around and pinch at the corners to make a waterproof boat for the paper cases.

4 Place the pan on the oven rack and pour boiling water into the pan, to half fill the space around the foil boat. Bake for 30 minutes. Leave to cool before serving.

Little Balls of Rice

Bolinhos de Arroz

This snack or appetizer is similar to one made in Italy (arancini di riso) *that uses cooked risotto rice, although this is lighter.* **Makes about 10**

1 Mix together all the ingredients in a bowl with a wooden spoon. On a floured board, shape into walnut-sized balls by pressing each one into a tablespoon, sprinkling with more flour as necessary.

2 Heat oil for deep-frying to 350°F, then fry the rice balls, a few at a time, until golden all over. Drain on paper towels and serve hot.

1¾ cups cooked long-grain white rice *cold*

1 free-range egg *beaten*

2 heaping tablespoons all-purpose flour

1 tablespoon milk

2 scallions *minced*

sprig of parsley or fresh cilantro *minced*

sea salt and freshly ground black pepper

oil for deep-frying

Chorizo Rolls

Enroladinhos

These are attractive salgadinhos *(appetizers), designed to be eaten in one bite with a cocktail. Ask your deli for a mild chorizo—or* chouriçou *in a Portuguese market— as there are many varieties.* **Makes about 40**

1 Wrap the bread in a damp dish towel and leave for 1 hour to ensure that the bread is elastic and pliable for rolling.

2 Remove the crusts from the bread slices.

3 Beat the egg yolks in a shallow dish with 1 teaspoon water and a seasoning of salt, pepper, and cayenne.

4 Dip each slice of bread in beaten egg to moisten, then roll it around a length of chorizo, pegging it in place with halved wooden toothpicks.

5 Cover the bottom of a frying pan with a film of oil and, when really hot, fry the rolls until golden all over. Remove and cut each one across into ½-inch lengths. Serve as part of mixed appetizers.

10 slices white bread

3 free-range egg yolks

sea salt and freshly ground black pepper

cayenne pepper

7 ounces chorizo

oil for frying

Shrimp Pastries

Empadinhas de Camarão

Empadinhas (or empadas) are the quintessential street food of Brazil, with various stuffings—spicy ground chicken, ham, cheese, vegetables, potato, and, especially, shrimp. Made with a short pastry, they are both appetizing and filling. **Makes 12–20**

For the pastry:

3⅓ cups all-purpose flour

½ teaspoon salt

1 cup (2 sticks) + 2 tablespoons butter or lard *softened but not melted*

2 free-range egg yolks

For the marinade:

juice of 1 lime

1 garlic clove *crushed, then chopped*

sea salt and freshly ground black pepper

For the filling:

6 ounces peeled shrimp, preferably raw *chopped if large*

olive oil for frying

1½ cups minced onions

1 green bell pepper *seeded and chopped*

8 ounces fresh ripe tomatoes *skinned and seeded* **or 1 x 16-ounce can whole tomatoes** *drained and seeded*

1 teaspoon tomato paste

sprig of fresh cilantro *minced*

1 teaspoon cornstarch

12 black olives *pitted and chopped*

1 To make the pastry, sift the flour and salt into a bowl and rub in the fat with your fingertips until the mixture is crumblike. Add one of the egg yolks and about 3 tablespoons water to bind to a stiff but kneadable dough. Roll into a ball, cover with plastic wrap, and chill for 1 hour.

2 Meanwhile, put the shrimp in a bowl with the lime juice, garlic, and some salt and pepper, and leave to marinate for 30 minutes.

3 Heat a little olive oil in a frying pan and cook the minced onions and bell pepper until softened. Add the tomatoes, tomato paste, and cilantro, and cook for a few more minutes to blend the flavors. Add the shrimp and their marinade to the frying pan and pour in enough water (up to half a wineglass) to moisten. Simmer for 10 minutes. Mix the cornstarch with 2 teaspoons cold water, add to the shrimp mixture, and stir until thickened. Add the olives, check the seasoning, and let cool.

4 Preheat the oven to 400°F. Meanwhile, roll out the pastry on a floured board to about ⅛-inch thickness. Using a 1½- to 2-inch pastry cutter, or the rim of a suitable glass, cut out 24–40 rounds. Place a heaping teaspoonful of the shrimp mixture on half of the pastry rounds, without overfilling them. Using a pastry brush, moisten the edges with water, then set another pastry round on top of each and pinch the edges with your thumb to seal. Beat the remaining egg yolk and brush over each pastry to glaze. Arrange on baking sheets and bake for about 20 minutes, or until golden brown. Serve hot.

Golden Fried Squid

Lula Frita

Squid can be disappointing if not cooked properly, for it very quickly toughens. It must be cooked for either a long time—up to 3 hours in a stew—to tenderize it, or, conversely, in less than a minute and served before it hardens up. Quick-fried squid can be served as bite-sized appetizers skewered on toothpicks. **Serves 4**

1 Clean the squid under running water, rubbing away any dark skin. Separate the tentacles, which can also be cooked. Slit open the pocket of the body and scrape away the inside with the back of a knife; discard. Rinse well. Cut the squid into 1- to 1½-inch squares. Mop dry on paper towels.

2 Shake some flour into a soup bowl and add a seasoning of salt, pepper, and cayenne.

3 Heat a thin layer of oil in a wide pan until very hot. Dip the squares of squid and the tentacles in the seasoned flour, and fry quickly until golden brown on both sides. (Cook them in batches rather than fill the pan, which would lower the temperature of the cooking oil.)

4 Drain on paper towels, squeeze lime juice on top, and serve with an optional dipping sauce of Chili Salsa.

2¼ pounds fresh squid

all-purpose flour for dredging

sea salt and freshly ground black pepper

cayenne pepper

oil for frying

juice of 1 lime

To serve:

Chili Salsa (see page 21) (optional)

Bean Cakes

Acarajé

These are the most renowned street snacks of northern Brazil, particularly in Bahia, where they are sold on the sidewalk by women in colorful costumes. Acarajé fritters have their origin in mainland Africa, but what makes these black-eyed pea cakes unique to Brazil is the addition of shrimp paste and chili to give an extra dimension of flavor and piquancy. If you find the smell of dried shrimp too pungent, you can omit it. The bean cakes will still be delicious. **Makes about 20**

1 pound (3 cups) dried black-eyed peas *slightly crushed in a food processor to split the skins, then soaked for at least 4 hours or overnight*

2 ounces dried shrimp

olive oil for frying

1 medium onion *coarsely chopped*

¼ teaspoon cayenne pepper or hot chili powder

sea salt

***dendê* oil for deep-frying (or use corn oil)**

To serve:

Chili Salsa (see page 21) (optional)

Coconut and Shrimp Cream (see page 79) (optional)

1 Drain the black-eyed peas, then put them in a bowl of water and rub them vigorously between your hands to remove the skins. Use several changes of water. The skins will rise to the surface and can be skimmed off and discarded. Finally, cover with very hot, but not boiling, water and leave to soak until cool enough for you to rub off any remaining skins.

2 Put the dried shrimp in a pan and cover with water. Bring to a boil, then simmer for 1 minute. Drain and rinse in cold water. Dry the shrimp on paper towels, then fry in a little olive oil for 1–2 minutes or until crisp. Chop roughly. In a blender or food processor, in small batches, purée the black-eyed peas, shrimp, and onion to make a thick paste. Season with the cayenne or chili powder and salt (carefully, as the shrimp may be salty). Heat a 3-inch layer of oil in a deep pan to 350°F.

3 Using a tablespoon, scoop up the paste and press into neat, compact oval shapes, smoothing them with your fingers. Deep-fry, in small batches of 5 or 6 at a time, for about 4 minutes, or until golden. After each batch, bring the temperature of the oil back to 350°F, and use a slotted spoon to skim off any detached crumbs of bean cake, which will otherwise burn. Drain the fried cakes on paper towels, and keep warm.

4 Serve whole or split open, with Chili Salsa or Coconut and Shrimp Cream.

Married Shrimp

Camarãos Casadinhos

One of the most attractive finger foods, this consists of two shrimp stuffed with cassava meal and skewered together, head to tail, with a wooden toothpick. **Serves 4**

16 large raw shrimp in shell, with heads

juice of 4–6 limes

1 garlic clove *crushed, then chopped*

2 teaspoons chopped fresh cilantro

sea salt and freshly ground black pepper

¼ cup cassava meal

pat of butter

sunflower oil for frying

To serve:

lime quarters

1 Remove the "whiskers" from the shrimp, but do not peel them or remove the heads. Mix together the lime juice, garlic, cilantro, and salt and pepper to taste in a bowl. Add the shrimp and toss to coat, then leave to marinate for 1 hour in a cool place. Drain and mop dry with paper towels.

2 Prepare the stuffing by heating the cassava meal in a frying pan, stirring in the butter, and cooking until the meal takes on a golden color (see Golden Cassava Meal, page 72). Remove from the heat.

3 With a sharp knife, make a deep incision lengthwise in each shrimp, to cut open the underside. Stuff with the cassava meal mixture. Using wooden toothpicks, skewer pairs of shrimp together, head to tail.

4 Fry in a shallow film of very hot oil for about 2 minutes on each side or until crisp and pink. Serve hot, garnished with quartered limes.

Spicy Stuffed Corn Husks

Abará

This is an ideal finger food, a neat envelope of corn husk (or folded banana leaf) enclosing a spicy filling. The filling is almost identical to Bean Cakes (page 30), though here it is steamed and not deep-fried. A similar dish, called acaçá, *where the filling is a paste of unseasoned white cornmeal mixed with ground shrimp, is eaten in honor of the deity Oxalá, known in Bahia as Candomblé, who is associated with voodoo rituals. Although not authentic, wax paper or even foil can be used to make the envelopes for steaming and the filling then transferred to lettuce leaves for serving.* **Serves 6 (makes 12)**

1 Soak the black-eyed peas in water overnight, or for at least 5 hours. Drain, then put into a bowl of fresh water. Rub the beans between your fingers to loosen the skins, which will float to the surface and can then be skimmed off. If the skins are resistant, pour boiling water over the beans and leave for 10 minutes before skinning. Drain the beans again.

2 Grind the beans in a blender, in batches, adding some of the oil to make them easier to blend. Transfer to a bowl.

3 Stirring with a wooden spoon, mix in the ground shrimp, onion, ginger, and salt to taste. Divide into 12 equal portions.

4 Plunge the corn husks or banana leaves into boiling water to soften them, then drain and pat dry. Roll a portion of the bean mixture between your palms to make an oblong, and wrap tightly in a corn husk or leaf. Tie closed with raffia or string (or use a rubber band). Make the remaining envelopes in the same way.

5 Place in a steamer, cover, and steam for 20 minutes. Cut the raffia or string before serving.

1¾ pounds (5½ cups) dried black-eyed peas

½ cup *dendê* oil (or use olive oil)

2 ounces dried shrimp *ground in a mortar or food processor*

1 onion *minced*

1-inch piece fresh ginger *peeled and grated*

sea salt

For the wrapping (optional):

fresh green corn husks or 12 pieces banana leaf *each about 6 inches square*

Lime-Marinated Fish

Ceviche

Ceviche *may well have developed from* escabeche *(page 36), in which poached or fried fish is marinated in an acidulated mixture.* Ceviche *uses the sour juice of limes or lemons to "cook" thin fillets of raw fish. Recipes for ceviche are found all along the coast of Brazil and throughout Latin America. It is especially good when the fish is perfectly fresh.* **Serves 4**

1 Cut the fish fillets into flat strips about 1 inch long.

2 To make the marinade, slit open the red chilies lengthwise and scrape out seeds and membranes. Chop into fine crescents. In a shallow dish, combine the chilies, lime or lemon juice, onion, garlic, cilantro, and a seasoning of salt and pepper. Toss the fish strips in this mixture, then leave to marinate in the refrigerator for at least 30 minutes, or until the fish turns opaque. Do not marinate for longer than 2 hours.

3 Drain the fish, discarding the marinade, and mix with the diced tomato. Serve with a decorative garnish of quartered limes, cilantro leaves, whole red and green chilies, and chopped scallions.

1 pound fillets of fresh sea bass or other fine-quality fish

1 large tomato *skinned, seeded, and diced*

For the marinade:

2 fresh hot red chili peppers

juice of 4 limes or lemons, or some of each

1 mild red onion or the white parts of 1 bunch of scallions *thinly sliced*

1 garlic clove *crushed, then chopped*

2 sprigs of fresh cilantro *chopped*

sea salt and freshly ground black pepper

To serve:

lime quarters

1 sprig of fresh cilantro *leaves kept whole*

4 fresh hot chili peppers (2 green and 2 red)

2 scallions *both white and green roughly chopped*

Soused Fish

Escabeche

The Portuguese and Spanish brought escabeche *to Latin America. This dish of fried fish pickled in a cooked vinegar marinade is not only tasty, it is an effective form of preservation in hot countries. It was developed by the Arabs who used the technique for meat and fowl as well as for all sorts of fish, such as tuna, anchovies, and sardines. A northern European form is soused herring. In Latin America, the pompano fish is often used.* **Serves 6**

6 fresh sardines *cleaned but heads left on* **(or use fillets of other oily fish such as mackerel, herring, or even farmed salmon)**

cassava meal (or use fine cornmeal or all-purpose flour)

4 tablespoons olive or sunflower oil

1 onion *minced*

2 garlic cloves *crushed, then chopped*

½ cup red wine vinegar

juice of 1 lime

1 bay leaf

6 black peppercorns

sea salt

1 Wipe the fish, dust with cassava meal, and fry in hot oil for about 2 minutes on each side until firm. Remove with a slotted spoon and set aside.

2 In the oil left in the pan, fry the onion over medium heat until soft but not brown. Add the garlic and cook for 1 more minute. Pour in the vinegar, ½ cup water, and the lime juice, and add the bay leaf and peppercorns. Simmer gently for 10 minutes. Taste and add salt if required.

3 Return the fish to the pan and heat through, then transfer, with the vinegar marinade, to a suitable dish or bowl and leave to cool. Store in the refrigerator for 24 hours or, preferably, 48 hours before serving. Fish preserved in this way will keep for a month at least if totally immersed in the marinade, with a film of olive or vegetable oil on top, and kept in the refrigerator in a sealed container.

4 Remove the fish from the marinade to serve.

Cashew Nut Toasts

Torradinhas de Castanho de Cajú

Cashew nuts, the harvest of northeastern Brazil, are used in many dishes. Here they are the garnish for a typical salgadinho, *or savory appetizer.* **Serves 6**

1 Preheat the oven to 400°F.

2 Toast the slices of bread, then remove the crusts and cut into quarters.

3 In a bowl, mix together the grated cheese, scallion, paprika, and a seasoning of salt and pepper.

4 With a metal spatula or broad-bladed knife, spread the cheese mixture onto the toasts evenly. Arrange on an oiled baking sheet and bake for 10–15 minutes. Once the cheese has melted, remove from the oven and sprinkle with the cashew nuts. Return to the oven to crisp up. Serve hot.

6 slices white bread

½ cup grated mild cheese such as *Minas Gerais* (or use Monterey Jack)

1 tablespoon minced white of scallion

1 teaspoon paprika

sea salt and freshly ground black pepper

2 tablespoons roughly chopped cashew nuts

Salt Cod Savories

Bolinhos de Bacalhau

Bacalhau, *or salt cod, is an abiding flavor of Brazil, first introduced by Portuguese colonizers, and ever present on menus today, not least as street food.* **Serves 6**

12 ounces salt cod
cut from the thick part

1 pound potatoes

**2 teaspoons chopped
fresh parsley**

**1 bunch of scallions, white parts
only** *minced*

4 free-range eggs *separated*

freshly ground black pepper

all-purpose flour

corn oil for deep-frying

1 Soak the salt cod in cold water overnight, changing the water several times. Put in a saucepan, cover with fresh water, and simmer for about 5 minutes, or until soft. Drain. When cool enough to handle, remove the bones carefully and mince the flesh.

2 Cook the potatoes whole, in their skins, in boiling salted water. Drain, then peel and mash (not with milk or butter).

3 In a bowl, beat together the mashed potatoes, salt cod, parsley, and scallions. Beat in the egg yolks one at a time until smooth. Season with pepper. If the mixture is slack, add a little flour to make it stiffer.

4 Heat a pan of corn oil to deep-frying temperature (about 350°F).

5 Beat the egg whites until stiff, and fold into the salt cod mixture.

6 Using a spoon dipped in flour, gently shape spoonfuls of the mixture into balls no larger than an egg. Deep-fry them, a few at a time, for 3–4 minutes or until golden all over. Remove with a slotted spoon and drain on paper towels. Serve at once.

Creamy Cod Savories

Torradinhas de Bacalhau

Torradinha is the name given to savory toasts offered as appetizers. These often consist of squares of toast topped with bacon, salami, and sausage, finished in the oven. Other toppings may be a dollop of mayonnaise with a peeled shrimp on top or a purée of tuna blended with mayonnaise. This recipe uses a savory purée of fresh cod with egg. A more pungent version can be made with dried salt cod that has been soaked overnight in several changes of cold water, simmered, and the bones carefully removed. **Serves 6**

1 Preheat the oven to 400°F.

2 Heat the oil in a frying pan and cook the onions gently until soft and changing color, but not browned.

3 Add the cod steak (or cooked salt cod) with the parsley and cook gently until done, when it will break into flakes. Take the fish from the pan and, when cool enough to handle, remove the bones carefully, along with any skin. Mince the flesh. Return to the pan and stir well into the cooked onions. Heat through.

4 Pour in the beaten eggs and season well. Stir until the mixture begins to firm up.

5 Spread out the squares of bread on an oiled baking sheet. Top each with a spoonful of the cod and egg mixture. Bake for 10–15 minutes, or until thoroughly heated and crisp. Serve hot.

3 tablespoons olive oil

2 medium onions *minced*

4 ounces cod steak or cooked dried salt cod

1 tablespoon chopped fresh parsley

6 free-range eggs *lightly beaten*

sea salt and freshly ground black pepper

6 slices white bread
each cut into four

MAIN
DISHES

Black Beans

Feijão

Beans and rice are the universal staples of the Latin-American world, especially in Brazil, the world's major grower of beans. The most popular bean is the small black one, often known as the turtle bean. Every family has its own way of preparing and flavoring them, adding a little bacon, fried onion, chili, sausage, or tomato to taste. Some beans are always taken out and crushed with a wooden spoon to thicken the sauce. Sometimes all the beans are crushed, to produce a thick purée, which is more digestible than the whole beans. Soaking and cooking times for the beans depend on their age; at a good grocery store with a steady turnover you may expect them to be freshest. **Serves 6–8**

1 pound (2½ cups) dried black beans

chunk of smoked bacon or ham bone (optional)

1 onion *minced*

4 tablespoons lard or bacon fat for frying

1 garlic clove *crushed, then chopped*

2-inch piece *lingüiça* **or chorizo**

1 bay leaf

sea salt and freshly ground black pepper

1 Rinse the beans thoroughly and discard any discolored ones. Soak in water to cover for 6 hours.

2 Tip the beans and their soaking water into a large pan, adding more water to bring the level to 6 inches above the beans. Do not add salt at this stage, as it hardens the beans. Bring to a boil and boil rapidly for 10 minutes, then lower the heat. Simmer for 2–3 hours, or until the beans are soft. If using, add the bacon or bone after 1 hour. When necessary, add boiling water so that the beans do not dry out. The beans are done when you can take one out and crush it to a paste.

3 In a frying pan, sauté the onion in the lard or bacon fat for 10 minutes or until lightly colored. Add the garlic and cook for 1 more minute. Peel the skin from the sausage. Shred the sausage, then add to the pan with the bay leaf, and cook with the onion for 5 minutes.

4 Transfer two or three ladles of beans with some of their liquid to the frying pan. Using a wooden spoon, crush the beans to a purée. Season with salt and pepper. Add the bean and sausage mixture to the pan of beans. Cook for at least a further 15 minutes to blend all the flavors.

Mule Drivers' Beans

Feijão de Tropeira

One of three classic bean dishes in Brazil, this is still, believe it or not, cooked by mule drivers plying their timeless trade in the hinterlands of northern Brazil. They would use mulatinho *beans (literally "mule drivers' beans"), a kind of red kidney bean.* **Serves 6**

1 Soak the beans in cold water overnight. Soak the dried salted beef in another bowl of cold water, changing the water several times.

2 Drain the beans and salted beef and put them in a large pot with the salt pork or bacon. Cover with fresh water and cook for about 1½–2 hours or until the beans are very tender and easily mashed with a fork. (Cooking times will vary with the freshness of the beans.)

3 In a frying pan, fry the onion in the olive oil until soft and yellow. Add the chopped sausage, crushing with the back of a fork to mash it. Add a few ladlefuls of beans and crush them into the mixture to make a coarse purée. Add this to the pot of cooking beans and cook for a further 10 minutes, although you can leave it on low heat to simmer for much longer if you wish, replenishing the water as required.

4 To serve, remove the chunks of meat, cut into smaller pieces, and return to the pot of beans. Garnish with hard-boiled egg slices, chopped parsley, and crisp bacon.

1 pound (2¼ cups) dried red kidney beans

6-ounce chunk dried salted beef (*carne de sol*)

3-ounce chunk salt pork or slab bacon

1 onion *chopped*

1 tablespoon olive oil

6 ounces chorizo or *lingüiça* *chopped*

To garnish:

4 hard-boiled free-range eggs *sliced*

sprig of fresh parsley *chopped*

strips of bacon *fried until crisp*

The National Dish
Feijoada Completa

The most familiar dish in the country, feijoada completa *is the daily staple dressed in its Sunday best or, to be precise, Saturday best, for that is the day it appears on menus throughout Brazil. This dish really needs the small black beans of Brazil,* feijão preto, *and you should use as many varied meats as you can—this recipe includes about 3½ pounds in all. Typical accompaniments are steaming white rice, Crisp Stir-Fried Kale (page 73), toasted Golden Cassava Meal (page 72),* malagueta *chili sauce or Chili Salsa made with some of the bean liquid (page 21), and slices of orange. And, of course, a glass of ice-cold* cachaça, *the spirit made from cane sugar.* **Serves 6**

1 pound (2½ cups) dried black beans

1 pound beef for stew (half could be sun-dried salted beef)

2 pig's feet (plus optional bits such as ears, tail, and, especially, salted tongue)

8 ounces smoked pork spareribs

6-ounce chunk slab bacon

1 large tomato *skinned and seeded*

1 tablespoon tomato paste

1 bay leaf

sea salt and freshly ground black pepper

1 onion *minced*

1 tablespoon vegetable oil

6 ounces chorizo *chopped*

2 garlic cloves *crushed, then chopped*

bunch of scallions, white parts only *chopped*

1 fresh hot green chili pepper *seeded* **(optional)**

1 Rinse the beans, then soak in water overnight. Soak any salted meats overnight, changing the water several times, to reduce salt content.

2 Use two large pans. Put the drained beans in one pan and the meat (except the chorizo) in the other, along with the tomato, tomato paste, bay leaf, salt, and pepper. Cover with fresh water and bring to a boil, then turn down to a simmer. Cook for 1 hour (both need skimming in the early stages). Drain the meats and add them to the pan of beans. Continue to cook for 30 minutes, or until the beans are mushy (the beans and meat should cook in about the same time).

3 In a frying pan, cook the onion in the oil until it is soft and golden. Add the chorizo, garlic, scallions, and chili, if using. Ladle some beans from the cooking pot with their liquid into the frying pan. Mash well, then add this coarse purée to the bean pan, to thicken the cooking liquid. Simmer for at least 10 minutes to blend the flavors.

4 To serve, remove all the meats, slice each nicely into six pieces, so that each guest will get a variety, and arrange on a large platter. Moisten with some of the cooking liquid. Serve the beans alongside.

Stuffed Cabbage Parcels

Trouxinhas de Repolho

Here is a dish with a European touch, similar recipes being found in peasant communities in France, Italy, Spain, and Portugal. **Serves 4 as a light lunch course**

12 leaves from a large head savoy cabbage *hard core removed*

1 medium onion *chopped*

4 tablespoons olive oil

4 garlic cloves *crushed, then chopped*

1 pound ground pork

sea salt and freshly ground black pepper

1⅓ cups long-grain white rice

8 ounces fresh tomatoes *skinned, seeded, and chopped* **(about 1½ cups) or 1 x 16-ounce can whole tomatoes** *drained and seeded, juice reserved*

1 tablespoon tomato paste

1 In a large pan of boiling water, blanch the cabbage leaves for a few minutes to soften. Plunge into cold water, then drain. Set aside.

2 Fry the onion in 2 tablespoons of the olive oil until soft but not brown. Add 3 of the garlic cloves and cook for 1 more minute. Stir in the pork and cook until it loses its raw color. Season. Remove from the heat and leave until cool enough to handle. Mix in the uncooked rice.

3 In a saucepan, fry the remaining garlic in the remaining 2 tablespoons olive oil for 1 minute, without browning. Add the tomatoes, tomato paste, and 2 cups water. (If using canned tomatoes, measure the reserved tomato juice and add enough water to make up the required amount.) Simmer for 5 minutes.

4 Spread out the cabbage leaves on a work surface. Spoon some of the pork and rice mixture into the middle of each leaf and wrap up into a tidy, small parcel. Pack into the bottom of a wide saucepan, with the folds underneath.

5 Cover with the tomato sauce and bring to a boil. Turn down the heat, cover with a lid, and, preferably using a heat diffuser, simmer gently for 45 minutes. Check the liquid level from time to time and add a little boiling water as required.

Chopped Steak

Picadinhos de Carne

This is probably the most common meat dish in all Brazil. To make it successfully it is important not to use ground beef or even best ground round—you need to buy a good cut of steak, which you then chop to a ground-meat texture. This will retain the juiciness of the meat. Don't use a food processor or a meat grinder, as they squeeze out all the liquid content, giving the meat a cardboard-like texture when cooked. Serve with Brazilian Rice (page 76) and peas. **Serves 4**

1 Trim the steak to remove fat and any gristle. Using a sharp, broad-bladed knife on a chopping board, mince the steak to a ground texture. It is a matter of taste how finely you mince the meat—the finer it is, the richer the sauce; the thicker it is, the juicier the meat.

2 In a frying pan, heat a film of olive oil and fry the bacon until the fat runs. Add the onion and fry until soft but not brown.

3 Add the minced steak and stir over the heat until it changes color. Season. Stir in the tomatoes and cook for a few more minutes. Pour in enough water to cover and simmer for 30 minutes, stirring from time to time, until the meat is well cooked and the sauce is a thick reduction. Add more water if it becomes too dry.

1¾ pounds boneless sirloin or rump steak

olive oil for frying

4 ounces slab bacon *rind removed, then cut into dice*

1 onion *minced*

sea salt and freshly ground black pepper

8 ounces tomatoes *skinned, seeded, and chopped* **(about 1½ cups)**

Meatballs in Tomato Sauce

Almondegas com Molho de Tomate

São Paulo, with its huge immigrant community, may owe this dish to the Italians who were first to settle there, back in the 1860s. It is an abiding favorite that has stood the test of time. You can use pork, or even lamb or chicken, instead of beef. **Serves 4–6**

1 Crumble the bread into a bowl and moisten with the milk. With a wooden spoon, beat in the eggs to produce a smooth paste.

2 Add the beef, onion, garlic, and a seasoning of salt and pepper. With your hands, mix well together and then shape the mixture into even-sized balls, no more than 2 inches in diameter. Dust the meatballs with flour.

3 Pour enough oil into a large frying pan to cover the bottom and heat until very hot. Fry the meatballs, in several batches if necessary, until well browned all over. Remove with a slotted spoon and drain on paper towels. Set aside.

4 Discard the fat and wipe out the pan, then cook the onion and garlic in a pat of butter for a few minutes or until soft. Add the tomatoes, the tomato paste, and seasoning. Cook until the mixture thickens, stirring to prevent sticking. Check the seasoning, then add the meatballs to the tomato sauce and cook together for a further 10 minutes.

5 Serve with steaming hot, boiled white rice.

4 slices white bread *crusts removed*

½ cup milk

2 free-range eggs

2¼ pounds ground beef or veal

1 large onion *chopped*

3 garlic cloves *crushed*

sea salt and freshly ground black pepper

all-purpose flour

oil for frying

For the sauce:

1 large onion *grated*

2 garlic cloves *crushed*

butter for frying

1¾ pounds fresh tomatoes *skinned, seeded, and chopped* **(about 4⅓ cups) or 2 x 16-ounce cans whole tomatoes** *drained and chopped*

2 teaspoons tomato paste

To serve:

boiled long-grain white rice

Grilled Meats
Churrasco à Gaucho

The churrascaria is a grill, and is particularly popular in the south, where there is plenty of meat. Whenever possible, large cuts of meat are roasted on a spit over the fire and then divided after cooking. Unique to Brazil is the method of rinsing the meat with brine as it cooks—this prevents the surface from hardening to the point where it can form a shield against heat penetration. Brazilians do not cut off fat from meat before grilling, for this both aids the cooking and adds to the flavor. Cut away surplus after cooking, by all means. For a party, the host will cook many cuts and types of meat, including chicken, pork, variety meats, and, especially, sausages. White meats—chicken and pork—are always marinated first, in a mixture of lime juice, minced onion and garlic, chopped parsley or cilantro, and seasoning to taste. Mop the meat dry before grilling. **Serves 4**

1 teaspoon coarse sea salt

2¼ pounds boneless beef sirloin or tenderloin, in one piece

1 Dissolve the salt in ½ cup boiling water, to make the brine for basting.

2 Make the fire. When the charcoal embers are red hot and the flames have died down, skewer the meat and put it in place over the charcoal.

3 Grill for 5 minutes on each side, occasionally brushing with the brine solution (use a pastry brush or, in more bucolic vein, a sprig of fresh rosemary or thyme). If the meat is cooked longer it will dry out and harden, but some prefer it so.

4 Remove the meat from the heat and leave to rest for a few minutes before slicing. Serve accompanied by salads, boiled long-grain white rice, Golden Cassava Meal (page 72), and a Chili Salsa (page 21).

Dried Beef Purée

Paçoca

Paçoca (pronounced pass-occa) is one of the chief dishes of Pernambuco, in the very north of Brazil, where the climate does not look kindly on the raising of cattle. Hence, the most common form of meat is carne de sol, *or salted meat (often the breast) dried in the sun.* Carne de sol *needs to be soaked to draw out the salt before cooking, after which it is pounded (another version of this meat when cooked is* velha roupa—*literally old rags, which is what the meat resembles when treated in this way). For* paçoca, *the cooked meat is mixed with cassava meal to make a nourishing and solid purée. In place of* carne de sol *you can use corned beef from a butcher.* **Serves 4–6**

1 Soak the dried salted beef in water to cover for 4–6 hours to draw out the salt, changing the water several times. Drain and mop dry. Cut into cubes about 1 inch across.

2 Cut the side pork into small dice. Cook them in a large frying pan over low heat until the fat runs. Add the beef and cook until golden brown. Remove the pork and beef with a slotted spoon and set aside. Using the same fat, cook the onions until soft and golden.

3 Combine the meat and onions and pound them in a mortar, to break up the meat into shreds. Or use a food processor, but don't overdo it.

4 Mix in the cassava meal gradually, to make a dense, smooth purée. Return to the frying pan and heat through, stirring. Season to taste. Serve hot with boiled rice.

1 pound dried salted beef (*carne de sol*)

8 ounces fresh side pork (belly)

4 onions *chopped*

2¼ pounds (8 cups) cassava meal

sea salt and freshly ground black pepper

To serve:

boiled long-grain white rice

Chicken and Shrimp Stew

Xinxim

Combining fowl and shellfish is typical of the cooking of northern Brazil. This classic dish is seasoned with dried shrimp and thickened with nuts. It is traditionally served with white rice, Coconut and Shrimp Cream (page 79), Golden Cassava Meal (page 72), and a chili sauce. Dried shrimp, although typical, have a pungent smell and can be omitted. **Serves 4**

3½-pound chicken *cut into 8 pieces*

juice of 3 limes

3 garlic cloves *crushed, then chopped*

sea salt and freshly ground black pepper

8 ounces peeled raw shrimp

sunflower oil for frying

1 onion *minced*

1 green bell pepper *seeded and minced*

2 large tomatoes *skinned, seeded, and chopped*

1 cup chicken stock

1 ounce dried shrimp

3 heaping tablespoons cashew nuts

3 heaping tablespoons shelled peanuts *toasted and skins rubbed off*

½-inch piece fresh ginger *peeled and grated*

2 tablespoons *dendê* oil

½ cup first-pressing coconut milk (see page 13)

sprig of fresh cilantro

1 Put the chicken pieces in a bowl, add one-third of the lime juice and garlic, and season. Toss, then leave to marinate for 30 minutes. In another bowl, mix together the fresh shrimp, half of the remaining lime juice and garlic, and seasoning, and leave to marinate for 15 minutes.

2 Dry the shrimp with paper towels, then fry in 1 tablespoon of oil for a few minutes on each side or until pink. Remove and reserve. Add a little more oil to the pan, then dry the chicken pieces and fry until golden on each side. Remove and reserve.

3 Clean the pan, add a little fresh oil, and fry the onion until soft but not brown. Add the bell pepper and cook until it softens. Add the rest of the garlic and cook for 1 more minute without letting it brown. Add the tomatoes and heat through, then return the chicken pieces. Cover with the stock, bring to a boil, then cover, and simmer for 30 minutes, checking occasionally to make sure the chicken isn't sticking and that the liquid hasn't all evaporated (add a little boiling water if necessary).

4 With a mortar and pestle, or in an electric grinder, grind the dried shrimp and nuts to a powder. Stir into the chicken mixture along with the grated ginger. Heat through for 5 minutes, then check the seasoning.

5 Add the cooked shrimp, remaining lime juice, the *dendê* oil, and coconut milk, and heat through. Serve hot, garnished with cilantro.

Fish in Coconut Milk

Peixe ao Leite de Côco

This is one of the most typical ways of cooking fish in Brazil, and is used with almost every variety. The fish is usually marinated in this fashion. **Serves 4**

4 steaks of white fish such as cod (about 9 ounces each)

1 onion *diced small*

2 green bell peppers *seeded and diced*

2 tomatoes *skinned, seeded, and diced*

⅔ cup coconut milk (see page 13)

1 tablespoon tomato paste

1 tablespoon olive oil

For the marinade:

juice of 2 limes

2 garlic cloves *crushed, then chopped*

2 sprigs of fresh cilantro *chopped*

sea salt

1 Put the fish steaks in a bowl and add the ingredients for the marinade. Mix, then leave to marinate for 30 minutes.

2 Transfer the fish steaks and the marinade to a large pan, arranging them in one layer, and cover with the onion, green bell peppers, and tomatoes. Mix the coconut milk with the tomato paste and pour over the fish. Sprinkle with the olive oil and leave to sit for 15 minutes to allow the fish to absorb the flavors.

3 Set the pan over low heat and simmer for 25 minutes. Brazilians do not mind the fact that the fish becomes very firm when cooked in this way. If more tender fish is preferred, remove the fish from the pan after it has been sitting for 15 minutes and simmer the other ingredients for 15 minutes. Then put the fish back into the coconut-milk mixture to cook for 10–15 minutes.

Shrimp Stew

Moqueca de Camarão

Moqueca (pronounced mok-ekka) is the simple stew of the north, in which fresh sliced vegetables are stewed slowly in oil for 20 minutes before shrimp, fish, or other ingredients are added. The most authentic versions contain too much rich dendê *oil for non-Brazilian palates, so this recipe substitutes vegetable oil (use sunflower or peanut oil, or even olive oil), with a little* dendê *oil to finish, thus supplying both the typical orange color and distinctive flavor.* **Serves 4**

1 Simmer the vegetables in the olive oil over low heat until they soften and release their juices, about 20 minutes. Season to taste.

2 Add the shrimp and simmer for a further 5 minutes, shaking to ensure even cooking. Avoid overcooking. Add the *dendê* oil and stir.

3 Serve hot with plain white rice, and a bowl each of Chili Salsa and *malagueta* chili.

2 large tomatoes *skinned, seeded, and sliced*

2 bell peppers (1 red and 1 green) *seeded and thinly sliced*

1 large mild onion *thinly sliced lengthwise*

7 tablespoons olive oil

sea salt and freshly ground black pepper

1½ pounds peeled raw shrimp

4 tablespoons *dendê* oil

To serve:

boiled long-grain white rice

Chili Salsa (see page 21)

***malagueta* chili**

Stuffed Crab

Casquinhos Recheados

This is one of the most popular dishes from northern Brazil, where seafood is abundant. It is commonly made with smallish crabs, about 3 inches across, but this is not vital for success. **Serves 4**

1 Mix the lime juice with the crab meat, and season with salt and pepper. Leave to marinate for 30 minutes.

2 Cook the onion gently in the oil until it softens. Add the crab meat, tomatoes, parsley, and Tabasco. Cook for a few minutes to blend the flavors, stirring and moistening with a little water to prevent it from sticking. Stir in the cornstarch mixture and continue cooking for a few more minutes to thicken.

3 Preheat the oven to 400°F.

4 Fill the scrubbed crab shells with the crab-meat stuffing and sprinkle with the grated cheese. Set on a baking sheet and bake for 10 minutes or until the cheese begins to bubble and brown. Serve at once.

juice of 2 limes

4 medium-sized crabs *meat removed and shells retained*

sea salt and freshly ground black pepper

1 onion *minced*

4 tablespoons sunflower oil

2 large tomatoes *skinned, seeded, and chopped*

sprig of fresh parsley *chopped*

splash of Tabasco or other chili sauce

1 teaspoon cornstarch *mixed with 1 tablespoon cold water*

1 cup freshly grated Parmesan or Cheddar cheese

Shrimp Frittata

Frigideira de Camarão

This is similar to the Italian frittata, an oven-baked flat omelet. A frigideira *though, in spite of the way it sounds, is not a cold dish, the* frigideira *being a heavy iron frying pan that can be used equally on top of the stove or in the oven. Unusually, baking powder is mixed with the beaten eggs. A deliciously savory* frigideira *is also made with salt cod (de-salted by soaking overnight), cooked as below, or rehydrated* carne de sol *(salted dried meat) or even green cashew nuts.* **Serves 4**

1 pound peeled raw shrimp

1 onion *minced*

1 green bell pepper *seeded and diced*

olive oil for frying

1 large tomato *skinned, seeded, and diced*

2 sprigs of fresh cilantro *chopped*

3 tablespoons first-pressing coconut milk (see page 13)

butter for greasing

6 free-range eggs

½ teaspoon baking powder

For the marinade:

juice of 1 lime

2 garlic cloves *crushed, then chopped*

sea salt and freshly ground black pepper

To serve:

boiled long-grain white rice

1 Preheat the oven to 375°F.

2 Marinate the shrimp in the lime juice, garlic, salt, and pepper for 30 minutes.

3 Fry the onion and green bell pepper in a little olive oil until soft. Add the tomato, cilantro, and coconut milk, and simmer until the mixture begins to thicken.

4 Stir in the shrimp and heat through to incorporate the flavors.

5 Butter a baking dish of a suitable size (unless you have used an ovenproof iron frying pan) and transfer the shrimp mixture to it. Beat the eggs with the baking powder, adding salt to taste, and pour over the shrimp. Bake for 30–40 minutes or until set.

6 Serve with steaming hot, boiled white rice.

Mussel Stew

Moqueca de Sururú

This is a dish familiar the world over, but, inevitably, in Brazil it is enhanced by the sweet and sour flavors of coconut milk and lime juice. **Serves 4**

2¼ pounds mussels

2 cups thinly sliced onion

8 ounces tomatoes *skinned, seeded, and sliced*

4 sprigs of fresh cilantro *chopped*

2 garlic cloves *crushed, then chopped*

juice of 2 limes

1 cup coconut milk (see page 13)

7 tablespoons *dendê* oil (or use olive oil)

sea salt and freshly ground black pepper

To serve:

boiled long-grain white rice

Golden Cassava Meal (see page 72)

1 Rinse the mussels in cold water, discarding any that are open (they are dead), broken, or heavy (they may contain mud). If necessary, scrub with a brush. Holding the shells firmly between thumb and forefinger, tug off the hairy "beards."

2 Put the mussels in a large saucepan and add the onion, tomatoes, cilantro, garlic, lime juice, coconut milk, oil, and a seasoning of salt and pepper (when adding salt, allow for the fact that the liquor that will come from the mussels when they open is salty).

3 Put the pan on a fierce heat, cover with a lid, and cook rapidly until the mussels open—a matter of only a few minutes if the pan is sufficiently hot.

4 Serve in bowls accompanied by steaming hot, plain boiled rice and toasted cassava meal.

Okra and Peanut Stew

Caruru

Caruru, from the northeast, is one of the most African and most traditional of Brazilian dishes. It combines okra with both dried and fresh shrimp, and a thickening of peanuts and cashew nuts, to make a tasty, glutinous dish to serve with Coconut Rice (page 77). The dish is richer if you use fish stock rather than water. If you are peeling your own shrimp, reserve the shells and use them to make a stock: Fry them lightly in a little butter or oil, then simmer them, just covered with water, with ½ chopped onion, 1 garlic clove, a bay leaf, a few peppercorns, a pinch of paprika, and some fresh cilantro stems for 15 minutes; strain, squeezing all the juices from the shells. You can, of course, make a stock with fish bones instead of shrimp shells. Note that dried shrimp are very pungent and, although authentic, can be omitted. **Serves 4–6**

1 Trim the okra and chop into very small pieces. Sprinkle with the lemon juice and a little salt.

2 In a food processor (or with a mortar and pestle), first grind the nuts, and then the dried shrimp.

3 Heat the oil in a large frying pan and cook the onion on medium heat until it starts to turn yellow. Stir in the ground dried shrimp and nuts, and cook for a few more minutes.

4 Add the whole shrimp and the ginger and cook for a few minutes, then add the fish stock or water and the okra. Simmer for 30 minutes on the lowest heat, stirring to prevent sticking and adding more water to prevent the stew from drying out.

5 Depending on your tastes, add a few drops of *pimenta-de-cheiro* or a chili sauce such as Tabasco diluted with a little boiling water. Sprinkle with toasted cassava meal and serve with coconut rice.

2¼ pounds okra

juice of 1 lemon

sea salt and freshly ground black pepper

⅔ cup shelled peanuts (or use ⅓ cup peanuts and ⅓ cup cashew nuts) *lightly toasted and skins rubbed off*

4 ounces dried shrimp *chopped*

2 tablespoons *dendê* oil (or use sunflower oil)

1 onion *minced*

1 pound peeled raw shrimp

1 teaspoon grated fresh ginger

1 cup fish stock or water

***pimenta-de-cheiro* pickled in vinegar (or use Tabasco sauce)**

Golden Cassava Meal (see page 72)

Coconut Rice (see page 77)

Shellfish Savory Rice

Arroz de Marisco

This typical rice dish from the north has neither the sophistication of an Italian seafood risotto nor the intensity of a Spanish arroz marinera in which seafood flavors are absorbed while the rice is cooking. On the other hand, it has the merits of simplicity, depending mainly on the excellence of the shellfish used. **Serves 4**

1 Put the shrimp and crab meat in a bowl, and toss with half the lime juice, the cilantro, and a seasoning of salt and pepper.

2 In a frying pan, sauté the onion in a little olive oil until soft. Stir in the tomato and tomato paste. Add the shrimp and crab meat, and, when very hot, add the mussels and oysters (or clams). Cover and cook until all the shells open in the steam, which will take only a few minutes.

3 Add the rest of the lime juice and check seasoning. Stir in the cooked rice and heat through until it is steaming and has absorbed the flavors of the seafood.

8 ounces peeled raw shrimp

8 ounces white crab meat

juice of 2 limes

3 sprigs of fresh cilantro *chopped*

sea salt and freshly ground black pepper

1 onion *minced*

olive oil for frying

1 large tomato *skinned and seeded*

1 teaspoon tomato paste

20 mussels *scrubbed and bearded*

4 or 8 fresh oysters or clams in shell

4 cups boiled long-grain white rice *left to cool*

SIDE

DISHES

Purée of Brown Beans

Tutú à Mineira

This is the predominant dish of the Minas Gerais province, where it's eaten with all pork dishes, alongside plain white rice and the universal couve *greens (Crisp Stir-Fried Kale, page 73). You don't need a lot of dried beans, because they double in size as they soak.*
Serves up to 6

1 Put the beans in a saucepan and cover with fresh water. Bring to a boil, skimming off the scum that rises to the surface. (Don't add salt at this stage, as it would harden the beans.) Turn down the heat and simmer for about 2 hours, or until tender. Beans vary in cooking time with quality and age, so cook longer if still hard.

2 Meanwhile, in a frying pan, cook the onion in the oil until soft. Add the bell pepper and cook for a further 5 minutes. Add the garlic and cook for 1 minute. Stir in the tomatoes and cook for a few more minutes. Stir in the cassava meal along with 2 cups of the liquid the beans are cooking in. Mix to a smooth paste, adding seasoning to taste.

3 Using a slotted spoon, remove the beans from their cooking liquid (which you must reserve). Purée them in a blender, in batches, adding a little of the reserved liquid to make a smooth purée.

4 In a large pan, mix together the puréed beans and the cassava-meal mixture, adding enough bean cooking liquid to give a texture that is neither too stiff nor too soupy. Check the seasoning. Stand this pan in a larger pan of simmering water to prevent burning or sticking. Heat for 15 minutes so the flavors blend and the mixture thickens. You can leave it to simmer longer, but replenish the liquid as necessary.

5 Serve sprinkled with chopped cilantro and scallions.

1½ cups dried small Brazilian brown beans (or use kidney beans) *soaked overnight*

1 onion *minced*

2 tablespoons olive or sunflower oil

1 green bell pepper *seeded and chopped*

2 garlic cloves *crushed, then chopped*

2 tomatoes *skinned, seeded, and chopped*

¾ cup cassava meal

sea salt and freshly ground black pepper

To serve:

sprig of fresh cilantro *minced*

bunch of scallions *chopped*

Golden Cassava Meal

Farofa Amarela

The most widely used garnish in Brazil, this is sprinkled like toasted bread crumbs on meat dishes such as stews, Grilled Meats (page 52), and the National Dish (page 46). It has a nutty, appetizing taste. In the north, it mops up the savory gravies of fish stews such as mussel moqueca (page 64). Farofa amarela (also called farofa mantiega) is made from coarsely refined cassava meal that is toasted to a golden brown with a little dendê oil or butter to give it a yellow color. It is simply served in a saucer at the table for you to help yourself. Ambitious cooks often add other ingredients appropriate to what they are serving, such as frying shreds of bacon first, then cooking the cassava meal in the resulting fat. Cassava meal may be toasted with a beaten egg, which causes it to thicken into small lumps. Chopped raw onion may be added, or herbs with roast pork, or sliced bananas and dried fruit with a seafood dish, or ground dried shrimp as in the variation below. **Serves 6**

2 cups cassava meal

pinch of sea salt

**3 tablespoons *dendê* oil
or 4 tablespoons butter**

1 Heat a frying pan over medium heat. Add the cassava meal and salt, and stir with a wooden spoon until hot.

2 Stir in the *dendê* oil or butter and cook, stirring, for a few minutes, or until the cassava meal turns golden. Immediately tip it onto a cool plate to stop the toasting process.

Savory Cassava Meal

This is a more savory farofa to serve with a Bahian seafood stew or shellfish dish. In a frying pan, briskly cook ⅓ cup minced onion in 4 tablespoons dendê oil (or other oil or butter) for 5 minutes to soften it, stirring to prevent it from burning. Mix in 2 cups cassava meal and 1 ounce ground dried shrimp, and stir together well, cooking until the cassava meal takes on a golden color. Remove to a serving plate or saucer. Note that to some tastes dried shrimp can be very pungent.

Crisp Stir-Fried Kale

Couve

This bright green vegetable is an essential accompaniment to The National Dish (feijoada completa, page 46). Quick cooking to keep its bright color is important, as is the way it is finely shredded to retain a chewy texture. **Serves 6**

1 Cut out the hard stems of the kale. Lay the flat leaves on top of each other and roll into a tight wad. Using a broad-bladed knife, cut across the roll into shreds no more than ¼ inch wide.

2 Heat the oil in a large frying pan, or, better still, a wok, and stir-fry the shredded leaves rapidly until tender but still chewy. They should keep their bright green color. Season to taste and serve.

1 pound curly kale (or use collard greens or Savoy cabbage)

2 tablespoons sunflower oil

sea salt and freshly ground black pepper

Stewed Green Papaya
Refogadinho de Mamão Verde

The mamão *is a larger version of a papaya, with brilliant orange flesh. Unripe, it can be cooked as a vegetable, gently stewed, which is what* refogadinho *means. You can use unripe papaya if you can't get* mamão. **Serves 4**

**1 large *mamão*
(or use 2 green papayas)**

1 onion *chopped*

oil for frying

2 garlic cloves *crushed, then chopped*

2 teaspoons tomato paste

sea salt and freshly ground black pepper

1 Peel the skin from the *mamão* or papaya, cut in half, and remove the large black seeds from the center. Prick the flesh with a fork and leave to soak in a bowl of water for 1 hour to remove some of the astringency in the flavor. Drain and reserve.

2 In a frying pan, sauté the onion in a little oil until soft and turning golden. Add the garlic and cook for another minute. Stir in the tomato paste and seasoning.

3 Cut the *mamão* or papaya into 1-inch pieces. Stir into the mixture in the pan, cover, and simmer for 5 minutes. Serve as a vegetable accompaniment with meat or chicken.

Brazilian Rice

Arroz a Brasileira

Plain boiled rice is the usual accompaniment for beans, but seasoned rice is often served. This is a typical dish. In Brazil, rice is not cooked drowning in water, but with just the right amount that will be totally absorbed. A rule of thumb is to use twice the volume of water to rice, e.g. 2 cups of water to 1 cup of rice. **Serves 4**

2 tablespoons sunflower oil

1 medium onion *minced*

1 garlic clove *crushed*

8 ounces fresh tomatoes *skinned and seeded* **or 1 x 16-ounce can whole tomatoes** *drained and seeded*

3 sprigs of fresh cilantro or parsley *chopped*

sea salt and freshly ground black pepper

2 cups long-grain white rice

1 In a frying pan, heat the oil until very hot. Add the onion, turn down the heat, and fry until it starts to color. Add the garlic and cook for 1 more minute without coloring.

2 Add the tomatoes, chopped herbs, and seasoning, and cook rapidly to evaporate excess moisture. Stir in the rice until well mixed.

3 Transfer to a saucepan. Add 4 cups water and bring to a boil. Then put on the lid (a crumpled piece of foil under the lid will stop steam escaping), turn to the lowest heat, and cook for 15 minutes. Use a heat diffuser to prevent burning, if necessary.

4 Remove from the heat and leave, still covered, for 10 minutes to continue cooking in its own steam, allowing the grains to separate. Remove the lid and allow the rice to dry out for a few more minutes before serving.

Coconut Rice

Arroz de Côco

This rice dish is eaten every day in many parts of Brazil to accompany meat, fish, or beans. You can use coconut milk that is freshly made, canned coconut milk, or that reconstituted from a powder. Alternatively, use 2 tablespoons grated from a bar of compressed coconut.

Serves 4

1 Bring 4 cups water to a boil, add the rice and salt to taste, and simmer with the lid off for 20 minutes.

2 Stir in the coconut milk and cook for a further 5 minutes, when all excess water should be absorbed or evaporated.

2 cups long-grain white rice

sea salt

4 tablespoons coconut milk (see page 13)

Coconut and Shrimp Cream

Vatapá

This is one of the national dishes of Brazil, combining the savory flavors of shrimp with smooth, sweet coconut and hot chili. It is bound together with crushed roasted almonds, cashews, or peanuts. Vatapá may be thickened with cassava meal or cornmeal, but it is more delicate if bread crumbs are used. If dried shrimp are too pungent for your taste, use 8 ounces peeled fresh shrimp and a few drops of Thai fish sauce (nam pla). **Serves 6**

1 Soak the bread crumbs in the first-pressing coconut milk for 30 minutes, then squeeze together to make a pulp.

2 Soak the dried shrimp in water to cover for 30 minutes. Drain and chop.

3 Heat a little oil in a frying pan and fry the onions over medium heat for about 10 minutes or until starting to color. Add the garlic and cook for 1 more minute without coloring.

4 In a blender or food processor (or electric coffee grinder), grind the nuts to a smooth paste. Remove, and then purée the dried shrimp with the green chilies. Add the ground nuts and the shrimp and chili purée to the frying pan, and fry with the onions for a few minutes, stirring well. Add the bay leaf, lime juice, and seasoning.

5 Pour in the second-pressing coconut milk and the fish stock, if using (you may not need to add all the liquid). Simmer, preferably over a heat diffuser, for 15 minutes or until thickened. Add the thick coconut cream and bread crumbs at the end, just heating through.

6 For a more substantial dish, add fish and/or shrimp, heating through until cooked.

⅔ cup bread crumbs from a day-old white loaf

5 tablespoons first-pressing coconut milk (see page 13)

4 ounces dried shrimp

dendê **oil (or use olive oil) for frying**

2 onions *minced*

2 garlic cloves *minced*

9 ounces mixed roasted almonds and cashews (half and half) or all roasted peanuts *skins rubbed off*

2 fresh hot green chili peppers *seeded and minced*

1 bay leaf

lime juice

sea salt and freshly ground black pepper

2½ cups second-pressing coconut milk (see page 13)

1¼ cups fish stock (optional)

2 fillets white fish, cooked and flaked (optional)

12 peeled cooked shrimp (optional)

Shrimp and Yam Purée

Bobó de Camarão

This smooth purée, colored bright orange due to the dendê *oil it is cooked in, is served on its own or as an accompaniment to meat or fish. It has its origins in Nigeria, and it is associated with a form of voodoo known as Candomblé. Bobó, also known as abobó, can be made with yams (as here)—not to be confused with sweet potatoes—cassava, breadfruit, or white beans. The use of cream makes it more luxurious. It is sometimes finished with a dusting of powdered dried shrimp that has been toasted in a dry frying pan.* **Serves 4**

1¾ **pounds yams** *peeled*

1 **onion** *grated*

dendê **oil (or use olive oil)**

2 **garlic cloves** *crushed, then chopped*

1-inch **piece fresh ginger** *peeled and grated*

8 **large raw shrimp (1¾ pounds)** *peeled and heads removed*

1 **pound fresh tomatoes** *skinned, seeded, and chopped* **(about 3 cups) or 1 x 16-ounce can whole tomatoes** *drained and seeded*

1 **teaspoon tomato paste**

1 **cup coconut milk (see page 13)**

1 **tablespoon chopped fresh cilantro or parsley**

freshly ground black pepper

4 **tablespoons whipping cream (optional)**

1 Cut the yam into 6 or 8 pieces. Cook in boiling water for about 20 minutes or until tender (test with a skewer). Remove with a slotted spoon to drain in a colander, reserving the cooking water.

2 When cool, purée the yam in batches in a blender (or use a potato ricer). Add a little of the cooking liquid if the mixture is too stiff. Set aside.

3 In a nonstick frying pan, fry the onion in a little oil on medium heat until soft. Add the garlic and ginger, and fry for 1 more minute. Add the shrimp and cook for 2 minutes on each side, or until pink and opaque. Remove and reserve the shrimp.

4 Add the tomatoes, tomato paste, coconut milk, cilantro, and pepper to taste to the pan. Simmer uncovered for 15 minutes, or until some of the moisture evaporates. Stir occasionally to prevent sticking.

5 Add the yam purée and cook for a few more minutes, stirring to a smooth consistency. Fold in the shrimp and, when hot, remove from the heat and stir in the cream.

Banana Bread

Pão de Banana

One of the delights of staying at an international hotel in Brazil is the promise of a breakfast feast. There is nothing grudging about the range of treats on offer, both savory and sweet, from fresh tropical fruit to savory specials, pastries, puddings, cakes, and fruit breads, none more delightful than banana bread. Yeast is not part of the baking tradition in Brazil, and many breads are made with baking powder as this one is. **Makes 1 loaf**

1 Preheat the oven to 350°F.

2 In a bowl, cream the butter with the sugar until thick and fluffy, then beat in the egg thoroughly.

3 In another bowl, mix the flour with the baking powder, salt, and nutmeg.

4 Mix some of the mashed banana and the vanilla extract into the egg and butter mixture, beating well. Then beat in some of the flour mixture. Continue adding the banana and the flour mixture alternately until everything is beaten in. Stir in the raisins and nuts.

5 Pour into a greased loaf pan that measures 9 by 5 inches. Bake for 1 hour. Test if the bread is cooked by inserting a metal skewer into the center: It should come out clean. Leave to cool in the pan for 15 minutes before unmolding onto a wire rack.

½ cup (1 stick) + 1 tablespoon unsalted butter *at room temperature*

2 tablespoons sugar

1 free-range egg *beaten*

1²/₃ cups all-purpose flour

1 tablespoon baking powder

pinch of salt

½ teaspoon grated nutmeg

3 large ripe bananas *mashed*

½ teaspoon pure vanilla extract

²/₃ cup raisins *dusted in flour*

3 tablespoons roughly chopped nuts (such as Brazil nuts or pecans)

Fried Plantains

Banana Comprida Frita

Plantains look like bananas and they are related, but they never ripen or sweeten, even when the skin changes color from green to black. As a starchy alternative to potatoes, they make excellent fries. They are also used in soups and sweetened to make a dessert. **Serves 4**

2 large plantains

oil or clarified butter for frying

1 It is not as easy to peel a plantain as a banana. Cut off the ends, then run the tip of a sharp knife along the ridges and pull the peel away. Cut the plantains in two, and divide each half into four, cutting lengthwise to make long fries.

2 Shallow fry in oil or clarified butter for a few minutes on each side until nicely browned. Serve hot.

Cheese Rolls

Pão de Queijo

The most universal, almost the most popular, form of bread, this is found everywhere. Some rolls are made with wheat flour, but this feather-light version uses tapioca flour, derived from the roots of the cassava plant. **Makes 12**

1 Preheat the oven to 450°F.

2 Sift the tapioca flour into a bowl. In a saucepan, combine the oil and salt with 6 tablespoons water and bring to a boil. Slowly pour onto the tapioca, stirring it to a stiff dough with a wooden spoon.

3 When the dough has cooled slightly, stir in the egg, then the yogurt and, finally, the cheese.

4 Grease your hands with an oily piece of paper towel, then form the dough into 12 balls. Arrange them on a nonstick baking sheet. Put into the oven and immediately reduce the temperature to 350°F. Bake for 25–30 minutes. You should be able to tell that the rolls are done by the appetizing smell, but you can test for doneness by inserting a skewer —if it comes out clean they are ready. Cool on a wire rack.

1²⁄₃ **cups tapioca flour**

4 tablespoons sunflower oil

generous pinch of sea salt

1 free-range egg *beaten*

6 tablespoons plain yogurt

½ cup freshly grated hard cheese, preferably Parmesan

Coconut Bread
Pão de Côco

Another tasty breakfast bread, but quite dense, this has the appearance of a flat cake.
Makes 2 loaves

2⅓ cups all-purpose flour

1 tablespoon baking powder

1 teaspoon salt

3 cups freshly grated coconut

6 tablespoons evaporated milk

1 free-range egg *beaten*

½ **cup (1 stick) + 1 tablespoon butter** *melted and cooled*

½ **cup + 2 tablespoons sugar**

½ **teaspoon pure vanilla extract**

1 Preheat the oven to 350°F.

2 Put the flour, baking powder, and salt into a large bowl and mix in the grated coconut.

3 Whisk the evaporated milk with the egg, melted butter, sugar, and vanilla extract until evenly mixed. Scoop out a well in the center of the flour and coconut mixture, and pour in the liquid. Beat well together to make a soft batter.

4 Divide the batter between 2 buttered loaf pans, each measuring 9 by 5 inches, filling them halfway. Bake for 50 minutes to 1 hour. Test if the bread is cooked by inserting a metal skewer into the center: It should not be sticky when you draw it out.

5 Remove from the oven and leave to cool in the pans for 10 minutes. Then unmold onto a wire rack to finish cooling.

Sweet Coconut Cornbread

Pão de Milho com Côco

The flavor of this cornbread is enhanced by the inclusion of grated coconut and coconut milk. **Makes 2 loaves**

1 Preheat the oven to 350°F.

2 In a large bowl, mix together the cornmeal, flour, sugar, salt, baking powder, and spices.

3 Whisk the eggs, milk, coconut milk, and butter together in another bowl. Gradually stir the liquid into the dry ingredients. Fold in the grated coconut, dried fruit and candied peel mixture, and lime zest.

4 Spoon the mixture into 2 greased loaf pans, each measuring 9 by 5 inches. Bake for 35–45 minutes. Test if the bread is cooked by inserting a skewer into the center: It should come out clean. Leave to cool in the pans for 15 minutes before unmolding onto a wire rack.

3 cups yellow cornmeal

¾ cup all-purpose flour

2 tablespoons sugar

1 teaspoon salt

2 tablespoons baking powder

½ teaspoon each ground cinnamon, cloves and grated nutmeg

4 free-range eggs *well beaten*

½ cup milk

½ cup coconut milk (see page 13)

¾ cup (1½ sticks) butter *melted*

3 cups freshly grated coconut (approximately 2 coconuts)

1½ cups mixed dried fruit (such as currants and raisins) and chopped candied peel *dusted with flour*

grated zest of 1 lime

Chayote Salad with Oranges
Salada de Xuxu

Among the most popular ingredients for salad is the chayote or xuxu *(pronounced shoe-shoe). It's a hard-skinned vegetable that's as green as a Granny Smith, and probably thinks it's a fruit, as it has large edible white seeds inside. It's bland to the taste, but what it lacks in flavor it makes up for with its fresh, juicy texture. Chayotes combine well with other vegetables and fruits, especially those with acidic flavors.* **Serves 4**

2 chayotes *peeled, seeded, and shredded on a grater*

3 oranges *peeled and sectioned (juice reserved)*

bunch of scallions, white parts only *chopped*

1 tablespoon extra virgin olive oil

juice of 2 limes

sea salt and freshly ground black pepper

To serve:

3 sprigs of fresh cilantro, parsley, or mint *chopped*

1 Mix the grated chayote with the orange sections and scallions in a bowl.

2 Make a dressing with the oil, lime juice, reserved orange juice, and a seasoning of salt and pepper. Add to the salad and mix everything together. Chill for at least 30 minutes.

3 Toss once more to mingle the flavors thoroughly, then serve with the herbs sprinkled on top.

DESSERTS
AND DRINKS

Avocado Cream

Creme de Abacate

Avocados provide almost instant, refreshing, and easy desserts. This is one of the most popular "sobremesas" in Brazil. **Serves 6–8**

3 ripe avocados

½ cup + 2 tablespoons sugar

juice of 1 lime

6 tablespoons milk

pinch of salt

3 tablespoons port wine

1 Halve the avocados lengthwise and remove the seeds. Spoon out the flesh from the skins, roughly chop, and put the pieces in a bowl. Sprinkle with the sugar and lime juice. Cover and chill for 15 minutes.

2 Place the avocado mixture in a blender or food processor with the milk and salt, and blend until smooth. Pass through a sieve, pressing with the back of a spoon.

3 Stir in the port. Heap into appropriate glasses and chill for at least 1 hour. Serve chilled.

Blancmange

Manjar

Manjar (which means no more than "eating" in Brazilian Portuguese) is short for manjar blanco. *It is a well-loved dessert in Brazil, its simple clean taste and texture providing contrast to the very many rich egg and coconut puddings.* **Serves 4–6**

1 In a saucepan, heat the milk with the rice flour, sugar, and salt, whisking to dissolve the sugar and incorporate the flour.

2 Before the mixture boils, remove the pan from the heat and set it in another larger pan half-filled with boiling water. On low heat, keeping the water simmering, cook for 15 minutes, stirring to make sure the mixture doesn't stick.

3 Pour into a buttered glass serving bowl. Leave to cool before transferring to the refrigerator to chill. Serve very cold with fruit conserves (*cocadas*).

5 cups milk

1⅓ cups rice flour

1 cup + 2 tablespoons sugar

tiny pinch of salt

To serve:

fruit conserves (*cocadas*)

Caramel Custard

Caramela

This is the most loved dessert in the Spanish- and Portuguese-speaking world, where it is otherwise known as flan. *Served chilled in small cups or soufflé dishes, it is found in every eating place, and sold off the street in outlets such as* leiterias *(milk shops). If you have a vanilla bean, heat it with the milk as you scald it, instead of using vanilla extract.*

Makes 8 individual custards or 1 large one serving 6–8

1 Preheat the oven to 325°F. Meanwhile, butter individual molds that are 2–3 inches across or one large mold.

2 In a nonstick saucepan, heat half the sugar, stirring with a wooden spoon until it melts and turns a deep brown. It must not burn. Pour a little melted sugar into each mold and tilt so that it spreads across the bottom.

3 Scald the milk by bringing it just up to boiling point, then remove from the heat and allow to cool. Add the vanilla extract.

4 In a bowl, beat the whole eggs and egg yolks with the remainder of the sugar until it has dissolved. Beat in the milk and salt.

5 Pour the mixture through a sieve into the molds (or large mold). Set the molds in a deep baking pan and add very hot water to the pan to come halfway up the sides of the molds. Bake for about 20 minutes, then turn down the temperature to 250°F and bake for a further 40 minutes. The custards are done when no liquid comes out if you press them. Or insert a knife blade, which should come out clean.

6 Leave to cool, then chill well. Before serving, invert each custard onto a plate. The sticky caramel mixture will have melted to make a delicious topping for this creamy treat.

butter for greasing

¾ cup + 2 tablespoons sugar

3 cups milk

1 teaspoon pure vanilla extract

2 whole free-range eggs

6 free-range egg yolks

tiny pinch of salt

Golden Milk Pudding

Ambrosia

A typically rich Brazilian dessert, this is often accompanied by homemade Coconut and Pumpkin Preserve (page 124). When cooked, the pudding turns a golden color and takes on a granular texture. **Serves 4–6**

1 quart milk

3 cups sugar

9 free-range egg yolks

1 Place the milk in a nonstick saucepan, or large nonstick frying pan, and bring to boiling point. Remove from the heat at once.

2 Add the sugar and stir to dissolve. Beat in the egg yolks one by one.

3 Using a heat diffuser, return the pan to low heat and leave to cook for 1 hour, stirring from time to time, until the mixture turns a delicate amber color and the texture becomes grainy.

4 Leave to cool before serving.

Sweet Cassava Cake

Bôlo de Aipim

Aipim *is one of two distinct kinds of cassava. The bitter cassava used for making meal first has to be processed to remove toxins, whereas* aipim *is ready to eat as a starchy vegetable, often boiled in chunks like potato. Once boiled it may be sliced into lengths and fried, to serve as an accompaniment to main courses. In this recipe, grated* aipim *is the basis of a cool-tasting fresh cake. You need a piece of* aipim *weighing 4½ pounds in order to get the required amount of flesh, after peeling, grating, and squeezing out moisture.* **Serves 6–8**

1 Preheat the oven to 350°F.

2 Peel the *aipim* and grate it (use the grater attachment on an electric mixer for preference, working in batches). Take handfuls of grated *aipim* between your hands and squeeze out as much surplus starch and water as you can. You should end up with about 3¼ pounds of grated flesh.

3 Put the grated *aipim* in a bowl and add the sugar, grated coconut, butter, egg yolk, and salt. Mix in as much coconut milk as is needed to make a creamy cake batter.

4 Make the glaze by dissolving the sugar in the coconut milk.

5 Butter a 9-inch cake pan, or a loaf pan, and pour the cake batter into it. Bake for 40 minutes, brushing at intervals with the sugar and coconut milk glaze. To test if the cake is cooked, insert a skewer into the center; it should come out clean.

6 Remove from the oven and leave to cool for 10 minutes before easing the cake out of its pan and onto a wire rack.

4½ pounds *aipim*

1 cup + 2 tablespoons sugar

⅔ cup freshly grated coconut

4 tablespoons butter *melted*

1 free-range egg yolk

pinch of salt

1½ cups coconut milk **(see page 13)**

butter for greasing

For the glaze:

1 tablespoon sugar

2 tablespoons coconut milk

Doraçy Cookies

Biscoitos de Doraçy

These are a feature of the Mato Grosso, the flat pampas lands in the middle of Brazil. The Mato is the equivalent of the bush in Australia. Although called cookies, these are more like little cakes, braided into a figure of eight with an extra twist, the ends linked to each other. They are fried golden brown, like a doughnut, and served with tea. **Makes 8**

1 free-range egg

1½ teaspoons sugar

1½ tablespoons butter *softened*

1⅔ cups all-purpose flour

1 package rapid-rise dry yeast

oil for deep-frying

1 In a bowl, beat the egg with the sugar until thick and creamy, then beat in the butter.

2 Sift the flour into a bowl, adding the yeast. Mix the flour and the egg and butter mixture together, kneading into a soft dough. You may need to add a teaspoon or two of water if too dry. Cut into 8 equal portions.

3 Shape each portion into a ball and roll out on a floured board into a thin sausage about 10 inches long. Take it by its two ends, cross it over to make a figure eight, and then make a second cross-over, pinching the end to seal. Cover with a cloth and leave to rise for 30 minutes.

4 Half fill a deep pan with cooking oil and heat until quite hot (about 330°F, not as hot as for French fries). Deep-fry the *biscoitos* four at a time, turning them over when brown on one side, to brown the other. Remove with a slotted spoon and drain on paper towels. Like doughnuts, these are best served hot.

Coconut Flan

Quindão

Coconut is the prime ingredient in literally dozens of Brazilian desserts for which the country is justly renowned. It was the Portuguese nuns who brought to Brazil the secrets of making egg-based desserts flavored with almonds. The workers from the slave plantations who learned these skills saw they could substitute coconut for almonds, and thus provide themselves with a living by selling the desserts on the streets. The quindão is a large flan; quindim are tiny ones, made by the same method. They are sold everywhere in Brazil today, especially in pastry shops as a tea-time treat. **Makes one 9-inch flan**

4 whole free-range eggs

4 free-range egg yolks

1 pound (4 cups) confectioners' sugar

3½ tablespoons butter *softened* **plus extra for greasing**

1¼ cups freshly grated coconut or dried shredded coconut

granulated sugar for dusting

1 Whisk the whole eggs and yolks until smooth. Beat in the confectioners' sugar, then add the butter and, finally, the grated coconut.

2 Preheat the oven to 350°F. Meanwhile, butter a nonstick tart pan, 9 inches in diameter, and dust it with a little granulated sugar. Pour the custard mixture into the pan. Set it in a roasting pan and pour enough hot water into the roasting pan to come just above halfway up the sides of the tart pan. Bake for 40 minutes, checking toward the end to see if the flan is done. The top should be dry, and a skewer inserted into the center should indicate whether it has set. If necessary, bake for an extra 10–15 minutes.

3 Leave to cool completely before attempting to unmold it. Loosen the edges with a metal spatula, then cover with an upturned plate and tip out the flan, upside down.

Note: Smaller flans (*quindim*) can be made in little individual tartlet pans and set in a roasting pan to bake, as above. They will take about 20 minutes to cook.

Sweet Potato Tart

Torta de Batata Doce

Brazilians are very fond of the sweet potato. It is used widely in soups, served as a vegetable accompaniment to main courses, and made into desserts. This very rich tart can also be made with pumpkin, the dense sort grown in the Americas (which can be bought as a purée in cans). **Serves 6–8**

1 Preheat the oven to 400°F. Set the sweet potatoes in a baking dish and bake for about 1 hour, or until soft. When cool enough to handle, peel and mash with a fork to make a purée. (If using pumpkin, bake in the same way.)

2 For the pastry, put the flour, sugar, baking powder, and butter in a food processor and process until the mixture resembles bread crumbs. Add the egg yolks and cream, and process to a smooth dough. Roll into a ball, wrap with plastic wrap, and chill for 30 minutes.

3 Preheat the oven to 375°F.

4 In a nonstick saucepan, heat the sweet potato purée with the sugar and coconut milk, stirring until the sugar dissolves. Remove from the heat and add the drained raisins, cinnamon, and vanilla extract. Leave to cool.

5 Roll out the pastry on a floured board and use to line a 10-inch tart pan or flan dish. Set on a baking sheet. With a metal spatula, spread the sweet potato mixture evenly in the pastry shell, then press in the chopped nuts. Bake for 25–30 minutes, or until the pastry is brown. Eat warm or cold.

2¼ pounds sweet potatoes

2 cups sugar

⅔ cup coconut milk (see page 13)

1 cup golden raisins *soaked in Madeira or sweet wine until plump*

2 teaspoons ground cinnamon

1 teaspoon pure vanilla extract

1¼ cups shelled peanuts, cashews, pecans, almonds, or Brazil nuts *skinned and coarsely chopped*

For the pastry:

1⅓ cups all-purpose flour

½ cup sugar

1 teaspoon baking powder

4 tablespoons butter *cubed*

1 free-range egg yolk

5 tablespoons whipping cream or crème fraîche

Heavenly Bacon

Toucinho de Céu

Strips of bacon describe the shape and color of these rich little desserts served in a caramelized syrup. Heavenly is how they taste. **Makes 20 or more**

1 In a large bowl, using a whisk, beat the egg yolks to a ribbon consistency, that is until the mixture thickens and lightens in color and comes away from the sides of the bowl in ribbons.

2 Butter a medium-sized heatproof bowl and pour in the egg mixture. Stand the bowl in a saucepan of water heated to simmering point, but not boiling. Allow to cook until the mixture firms to a jelly-like consistency without hardening completely, about 15–20 minutes. Remove from the pan of water and leave to cool completely. Then turn the egg mixture out of the bowl and cut into thin slices, like strips of bacon.

3 In a nonstick pan, heat 2 tablespoons of the sugar, stirring until it melts and caramelizes, turning an appetizing dark brown (but not blackening, which means it is burning). Remove from the heat at once and place the base of the pan in a bowl of cold water to arrest the cooking.

4 Return the pan to the heat and add 1 quart water, stirring to dissolve the caramel. Add the remaining sugar and dissolve it, then cook to a thick sugar syrup. Add the lemon zest and cinnamon. Simmer the syrup for 10 minutes.

5 Add the strips of egg yolk and simmer gently for 10 minutes or until they are well soaked. With a slotted spoon, remove them to a serving plate. Boil the remaining sugar syrup for 5–10 minutes to evaporate some of the moisture. Pour the thick syrup over the heavenly bacon and leave to cool. A sticky treat, served cold.

12 free-range egg yolks

butter for greasing

3¾ cups sugar

grated zest of ½ lemon

½ cinnamon stick

Mango Sorbet
Sorvete de Manga

*Mango, passion fruit (*maracujá*), pineapple (*abacaxi*), and guava (*goiaba*) all make the most delicious sorbets. But these are only a few of the many sorbet flavors offered in Brazilian cafés and restaurants—many more sorbets are made with unusual tropical fruits that are not exported.* **Serves 4–6**

1 cup sugar

4 ripe mangoes (about 1¾ pounds)

juice of 1 lime

1 Make a sugar syrup by dissolving the sugar in ½ cup water and bringing to a boil, stirring. Allow to cool completely.

2 Peel the mangoes and cut away the flesh from their flat seeds. Purée the flesh in a blender in batches, adding the lime juice.

3 Mix the purée into the sugar syrup. Freeze in an ice-cream machine, if you have one, following the manufacturer's instructions. Or pour into a shallow dish and put into the freezer; every 30 minutes remove the tray and beat the mixture with a fork or whisk to break up ice crystals as they form, then return to the freezer. Repeat this three or four times until the sorbet sets.

4 Remove the sorbet from the freezer to the refrigerator 20 minutes before serving.

Mother-in-Law's Eyes

Olhas de Sogra

Another evocatively named sweet, this consists of prunes stuffed with a coconut mixture, the filling representing the eyeball and pupil quite realistically. Olhas de sogra are often sold in sweet shops, where a bizarre, extremely realistic effect is achieved. It is possible to buy very good quality pitted prunes, but those from Agen in France have the best flavor. Serve with strong coffee (removing the clove before eating). **Makes about 30**

1 To make the filling, dissolve the granulated sugar in ½ cup boiling water. Off the heat, stir in the grated coconut. Beat in the egg yolks, one by one. Using a heat diffuser, return to the heat and stir until the mixture thickens. Remove and leave to cool.

2 Open up each prune to receive the stuffing, smoothing in a mixture of coconut filling to represent the eyeball. Artistically place a clove at the center of each to make the pupil of the mother-in-law's eye.

3 Dredge each sweet in a bowl of confectioners' sugar. Serve in paper bonbon cases.

1 cup granulated sugar

3 cups freshly grated coconut

2 free-range egg yolks

1¾ pounds large prunes
pits removed

whole cloves

confectioners' sugar for dredging

Students' Cakes

Bolinho de Estudante

Tapioca, one of the by-products of processing cassava, is used in both savories and desserts. These are easily made deep-fried cakes. **Makes about 12**

1½ **cups tapioca flour**

⅓ **cup granulated sugar**

⅔ **cup freshly grated coconut**

1 **cup milk**

pinch of salt

all-purpose flour for dusting

oil for deep-frying

ground cinnamon

confectioners' sugar

1 In a bowl, mix together the tapioca flour, granulated sugar, coconut, milk, and salt, then add enough water (about ½–1 cup) to make a smooth paste. Leave it to stand for 15 minutes.

2 Roll out on a floured board to ½-inch thickness. Use a small cup or glass to cut out disks about 2 inches across.

3 Deep-fry in hot oil at 350°F until golden brown on both sides. Drain on paper towels, then sprinkle with cinnamon and confectioners' sugar.

Angels' Cheeks

Papos de Anjo

Its name betrays its convent origins—this is one of many desserts deriving from the Portuguese nuns who first came to Brazil in the fifteenth century, bringing with them the skills in the making of egg and almond sweets learned from the Moors.

Makes 12 medium-sized cakes

2 free-range eggs *separated*

4 free-range egg yolks

2 tablespoons all-purpose flour

½ teaspoon baking powder

butter for greasing

For the sugar syrup:

1¼ cups sugar

½ teaspoon pure vanilla extract

1 Preheat the oven to 400°F.

2 In a bowl, whisk the 2 egg whites until firm, then beat in the 6 egg yolks one by one. Beat in the flour with the baking powder, and continue beating until the batter thickens.

3 Lightly butter a 12-hole muffin tray, each hole about 2½ inches across. Pour the batter into the holes to fill each to two-thirds. Bake for 20 minutes, checking if the cakes are cooked by inserting a skewer into the center; it should come out clean when you remove it. The cakes will puff up and turn a lovely golden color.

4 Dissolve the sugar in 1 cup water, then bring to a boil. Remove from the heat. When cool, add the vanilla extract.

5 When the cakes are cool, remove them from the muffin pans, place them in a suitable shallow dish, and pour the syrup over them, allowing it to soak in.

Dreams

Sonhos

These sweet desserts, made with polvinho *(tapioca flour), are typically Brazilian. They puff up when deep-fried, and are best eaten hot and crisp from the pan.* **Makes 12–16**

1 In a nonstick saucepan, heat the milk with the granulated sugar and salt, stirring to dissolve. As it bubbles to the boil, tip in all the tapioca flour, stirring with a wooden spoon. Remove from the heat at once and beat until the mixture leaves the side of the pan, forming a hot ball of dough.

2 Beat in the egg yolks one at a time, mixing throroughly before adding the next.

3 Heat a pan of oil for deep-frying to about 350°F. Using a large teaspoon, shape balls of the dough and fry, a few at a time, until golden on all sides.

4 Drain on paper towels, then roll in a saucer of confectioners' sugar mixed with cinnamon. Eat while hot.

1 cup milk

1 tablespoon granulated sugar

¼ teaspoon salt

scant 1 cup tapioca flour

4 free-range egg yolks

oil for deep-frying

2 tablespoons confectioners' sugar

1 teaspoon ground cinnamon

Longings

Saudades

How much is expressed in this simple word—perhaps longings of Portuguese immigrants for family and homeland? This is one of the simplest forms of the many hundreds of sweets made with egg yolks and sugar, and is like a cross between a macaroon and a meringue.
Makes 20

5 free-range egg yolks

1¼ cups sugar

1½ cups fine sago flour

1 Preheat the oven to its lowest setting.

2 In a mixing bowl, beat the egg yolks to the ribbon stage—until thick and light in color, and leaving the side of the bowl in ribbons. Beat in the sugar.

3 Pour in the flour bit by bit, mixing into a paste with a wooden spoon until you can use your hands for mixing. Add enough flour so that you can shape the paste into balls half the size of an egg.

4 Lay the balls on a baking sheet and put into the oven. Leave until well dried out, which can take several hours. The time needed depends on your oven.

Milk Sweet

Doce de Leite

This is a popular accompaniment to desserts, similar to clotted cream. It's sometimes eaten on bread or with cakes, and sometimes with a spoon just as it is. One common Latin-American version is made by immersing an unopened can of sweetened condensed milk in water and simmering for several hours, after which (taking care to let it cool thoroughly before opening) it will have turned to a soft toffee-like consistency. Doce de leite forms little lumps after prolonged cooking and so should be removed from the heat when it starts to brown. **Serves 6–8**

1 Put the milk and sugar in a saucepan and bring to a rapid boil, stirring with a wooden spoon until the sugar dissolves.

2 Add the vanilla bean and cinnamon. Turn down the heat to the lowest possible and simmer for about 1½ hours, stirring from time to time to prevent sticking.

3 As the water in the milk evaporates, the mixture thickens and reduces in volume. Eventually the dense sugars begin to brown and form lumps. Remove and discard the vanilla bean and cinnamon sticks. Take off the heat and leave to cool, then chill.

4 Serve chilled. *Doce de leite* will keep in the refrigerator for a week.

3 quarts milk

2¼ pounds (5 cups) sugar

1 vanilla bean

2 sticks cinnamon

Creamy Chocolate Fudge

Brigadeiro

This is one of the universal children's party sweets in Brazil.
Makes about 40 pieces

1 In a nonstick saucepan, over a heat diffuser, gently heat the condensed milk with the butter, chocolate, and milk. Stir with a wooden spoon until the mixture comes away from the sides of the pan.

2 Remove from the heat and add the vanilla extract.

3 On a cool buttered surface (a marble slab would be ideal), spread the mixture with a metal spatula.

4 When cool enough to handle, cut the mixture into 40 pieces. With your hands, roll each into a small ball and then roll in chocolate sprinkles to coat all over.

5 If you have suitable small candy molds, press the fudge in to shape the pieces. Lay them on a tray lined with wax paper and allow to cool thoroughly and set.

2 x 16-ounce cans condensed milk

1½ tablespoons unsalted butter

3 tablespoons grated semisweet chocolate

7 tablespoons milk

5 drops of pure vanilla extract

butter for greasing

chocolate sprinkles

Nut Brittle

Pé-de-Moleque

This is sold in towns and cities alike, but it is easy enough to make at home. Use other nuts to taste, such as chopped castanha de Pará *(Brazil nuts), almonds, or hazelnuts. This recipe uses the cheapest nuts—*amendoim, *or peanuts. Moist dark brown sugar gives a luscious, rich flavor, while white sugar lets the nuts speak for themselves.* Moleque *is a mischievous boy, urchin, or beggar, and his* pé *is his foot. So this is Ragamuffin's Foot.*

Makes about 2¼ pounds

1 pound unsalted peanuts

2 pounds (4½ cups packed) dark brown or Barbados sugar or white granulated sugar

butter for greasing

1 Toast the peanuts under the broiler or on low heat in a very lightly oiled frying pan. Keep shaking the nuts so that they toast evenly. If you cook them too quickly, they will burn on the outside, remaining raw inside.

2 Remove from the heat. When cool enough to handle, rub the nuts in a dish towel to loosen the flaky skins. Roughly chop the peanuts.

3 Bring 1 quart of water to a boil. Pour in the sugar, stirring until it dissolves. Boil rapidly and, when the syrup begins to thicken, add the peanuts. Continue boiling until the brittle is ready, stirring to prevent sticking. To test, remove a little with a wooden spoon and dip it into a bowl of cold water; if the brittle hardens, it is ready. If you have a candy thermometer, this should be the hard crack stage, 295°F.

4 While the brittle is boiling, half fill the sink with cold water. As soon as the brittle is ready, remove the pan from the heat and gently dip the base into the cold water for a few moments, to stop the cooking.

5 Pour the brittle onto two buttered flat pans, each about 12 by 8 inches. When almost cool, make cuts all over the surface to mark out roughly shaped pieces. When cold, break the brittle along these lines.

Passion Fruit Cocktail

Batida de Maracujá

The batida *is the cousin of the* caipirinha, *a chilled white rum cocktail made with freshly pressed fruit juice. The main difference between a lime* batida *and* caipirinha *is that the juice for the former is strained before serving.* Batidas *are made with every kind of fruit juice, from pineapple juice to coconut milk.* Maracujá *(passion fruit) is one of the most liked, evoking the heady scents of tropical Brazil.* **Makes 4 cocktails**

1 Cut the passion fruits in half and scoop out the flesh into a sieve. Press with the back of a spoon to strain the juice from the seeds. (The seeds and skins can be heated through with a glass of water and 1 tablespoon of sugar, then strained and cooled, to make a tart sauce that you can add to a fruit salad, or thicken with cornstarch to serve as a sauce.)

2 Slip the ice cubes into a small plastic bag, place on a chopping board, and reduce them to splinters using a rolling pin or similar.

3 Combine the *cachaça*, passion fruit juice, sugar, and crushed ice, and shake well.

4 Serve in glasses you have chilled in the freezer.

8 wrinkled passion fruits

20 ice cubes

1¼ cups *cachaça*

4 teaspoons superfine sugar

White Rum Sour

Caipirinha

The most famous of traditional Brazilian cocktails, this is drunk before a meal to give you a kick-start. The ice is cooling, the freshness of the lime arouses the appetite, and the concentration of alcohol animates conversation. Caipirinha *actually translates as "yokel" or "country bumpkin," perhaps indicating the rough and ready way the limes are coarsely chopped into the drink. There are literally hundreds of brands of* cachaça, *the national spirit, a white rum made from cane sugar, the best very good indeed. Modern twists are* caipirosca *with vodka instead of* cachaça, *and* caipirissima, *made with Bacardi rum.*

Makes 4 cocktails

2 limes

16 ice cubes

4 teaspoons superfine sugar

1¼ cups *cachaça*

1 With a sharp knife, cut the limes into quarters and remove the coarse central membranes. Slice the lime quarters into small, even chunks.

2 Put the ice cubes into a plastic bag, place on a chopping board, and reduce them to splinters using a rolling pin or similar.

3 Combine the limes and sugar in a mortar (skillful barmen do all this in individual glasses in front of you), pounding them together. Add the *cachaça* and crushed ice and shake well, preferably in a cocktail shaker or in a pitcher with the top covered. Don't use a blender—the pieces of lime must remain whole.

4 Serve in glasses you have chilled in the freezer.

Opposite *White Rum Sour and Passion Fruit Cocktail (page 119)*

Coconut Milk Shake

Refresco de Côco

Here is a deceptively simple, cooling, and nourishing drink for a hot day. This recipes uses skim milk, which is light and refreshing, although lowfat or whole milk is just as tasty, if more filling. **Makes 4 drinks**

1 coconut

1 quart skim milk

sugar to taste

1 Pierce two of the three holes at the base of the coconut and pour out the liquid (*água de côco*), reserving it. Strain the liquid in a sieve to remove fibers and dust that fall from the shell.

2 Break open the coconut using a hammer or other implement. Cut the shards of flesh from the shell. Cut the hard brown skin from the coconut flesh, then grate, using an electric mixer with a grater attachment to spare your fingers.

3 Heat the milk, without boiling, and stir in the grated coconut. Remove from the heat and put aside to infuse for 40 minutes. Pour the coconut-flavored milk through a cloth into a bowl, tightening the cloth to extract all the juice, like wringing out a shirt. Combine with the *água de côco*.

4 Add a little sugar to taste, stirring to dissolve, then add a little water to dilute the drink. Chill well. Serve with ice cubes.

Limeade

Limonada Suissa

Limonada suissa is the name given in Brazil to the national drink of limeade, the pungent green limão *being the nearest citrus fruit they have to lemon.* **Makes 6–8 drinks**

1 Pare the zest from 1 lime. Put the zest in a saucepan with the sugar and ½ cup water and bring to a boil, stirring until the sugar has dissolved. Remove from the heat and leave to cool completely. Remove the lime zest.

8 limes

1¼ cups sugar

2 Squeeze the juice from the limes and add to the sugar syrup. Chill.

3 Serve cold, adding crushed ice and water to dilute to taste.

Coconut and Pumpkin Preserve
Cocada com Abóbora

Brazil has many unconventional preserves not found elsewhere, such as sugared beets, sweetened carrot, and many based on pumpkin, a native vegetable. Unusually, pumpkin is combined with coconut in this preserve. **Makes about 2 x 1-pound jars**

about 9 ounces *abóbora* (or use butternut or kabocha squash)

2½ cups sugar

2 cloves

2 cups freshly grated coconut or 1½ cups dried shredded coconut

1 Peel the *abóbora* and remove the fibers and seeds. Cut the flesh into small pieces (you should have about 1¼ cups).

2 Bring 1 quart of water to a boil in a saucepan. Add the sugar and stir to dissolve.

3 Add the *abóbora* and the cloves. Quickly bring to a boil and cook until the *abóbora* breaks down into a purée, stirring to prevent sticking or burning. When it thickens, stir in the coconut and simmer for 10 more minutes to allow the coconut flavors to combine with the pumpkin.

Caramelized Coconut Preserve

Dissolve 3 cups sugar in 1 cup water. Off the heat, stir in 2 cups freshly grated coconut or 1½ cups dried shredded coconut, then simmer on low heat for 10 minutes. Leave to cool.

White Coconut Preserve

Make the Caramelized Coconut Preserve using milk instead of water and flavoring it with 2–3 cloves.

Guava Paste

Goiabada

The acidic, highly scented guava, varying from raw green to pretty yellow and pink, is a very popular fruit in Brazil, and is used in conserves, gelatin molds, mousses, and drinks. A thick jellied paste of guava is usually found on the breakfast table to be eaten with a slice of cheese, perhaps the squeaky, fresh white cheese of Minas Gerais. Goiabada is a cousin of the Spanish mermelada, or quince paste, which is also popular in Brazil.

Makes about 1 pound

1 Cut off the skins of the guavas and scrape out the seeds. Push the pulp through a fine sieve. You should be left with about 1 pound puréed pulp. Weigh out an equal amount of sugar.

2¼ pounds ripe guavas

sugar

butter for greasing

2 Put the sugar in a large pan and add ½ cup water. Bring to a boil, stirring to dissolve the sugar, then boil to the soft ball stage (239°F on a candy thermometer). You can test by dipping a teaspoon of the boiling sugar syrup into a bowl of cold water; if the syrup can be shaped into a small ball, it is ready.

3 Add the guava purée and stir with the sugar syrup until the mixture comes away from the sides of the pan. Remove from the heat. Spread out in a buttered baking pan and leave to cool.

4 Once cold and set, cut into squares and wrap in wax paper to store in airtight tins.

Page numbers in *italic* refer to the illustrations

I would like to thank the many Brazilian friends who have, over the years, shared with me their love of Brazil, and introduced me to its vibrant culture: in particular, Marcia Magnavita Marques da Silva and her family; Betty Chiaratti, Margaret van Peterkin, and David and Zelia Edwards. Among others who have offered inspiration and information: chef Jean-Yves Poirey and Teresa Pedruzzi of Le Meridien, Copacabana, Rio de Janeiro, and chef Adauto Rodrigues of the São Paulo Hilton; in London, Andrew and Alberina Hunton of Sabor do Brasil, Highgate; at the Brazilian Embassy in London, Tovar da S. Nunes and Maria Graça-Fish.

I owe a special debt to Elisabeth Lambert Ortiz, the food writer most influential in awakening us to the Latin-American culinary world in books such as *The Book of Latin-American Cooking* (Penguin) and *The Flavours of Latin America* (Latin-American Bureau, London). Among Brazilian books that convey the unique spirit of the Northeast are *A Culinaria Baiana*, produced by the SENAC cooking school in Salvador de Bahia, and Darwin Brandão's *A Cozinha Baiana*.

I would also like to thank the Conran Octopus team for their warm support, managing editor Kate Bell, art director Leslie Harrington and copy editor Norma MacMillan, as well as Suzannah Gough and Jenni Muir, who first invited me to write this book.

And finally, thanks to my wife, Heather, and my children, Alex and Georgia, who share my passion for all things Brazilian.

PUBLISHER'S ACKNOWLEDGMENTS

The publisher would like to thank the following photographers for their kind permission to reproduce the photographs in this book:

6–7 James Davis Travel Photography; 38–39 Anthony Blake Photo Library/Guy Moberly; 60–61 Travel Ink/Charlie Marsden; 84–85 Carlos Freire/Hutchison Library; 112–113 Sue Cunningham/SCP

Also thanks to Hilary Bird, Helen Ridge, Susanna Tee, and Sarah Widdecombe.